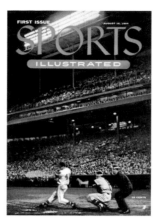

INAUGURAL ISSUE
AUGUST 16, 1954

Sports Illustrated
The COVERS

Sports Illustrated
The COVERS

25 CENTS

ROGER BANNISTER: SPORTSMAN OF THE YEAR

SPORTS ILLUSTRATED

JANUARY 3, 1955
25 CENTS

Contents

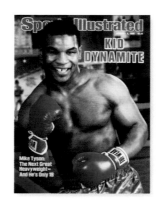

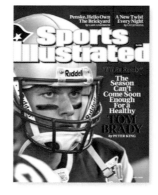

Editor / GREG KELLY   *Designer /* STEVEN HOFFMAN   *Associate Designers /* JOSH DENKIN, LINDA TRAN TUTOVAN   *Photo Editor /* CRISTINA SCALET
Copy Editor / KEVIN KERR   *Reporter /* ADAM CAPARELL   *Research Assistant /* LILY FINE   *Project Manager /* STEFANIE KAUFMAN

The Cover Story

BY TERRY McDONELL

THE COVER IS THE FACE OF any magazine, the first thing readers see, the place where the editors declare their intentions. At SPORTS ILLUSTRATED the cover has inspired keen interest bordering on obsession since late 1953, when Sid James, the magazine's first managing editor, struggled over which images to use on the two dummy issues he was putting together for prospective advertisers to help determine whether the country wanted or needed a sports weekly at all.

The cover photograph on the first dummy issue was a shot of the crowd at Oklahoma's rainy November football victory over Nebraska. The absence of football action underlined the basic SPORTS ILLUSTRATED proposition: that a new leisure class with a growing interest in recreation was a market waiting to happen. The second dummy cover showed a golfer, framed by spectators, teeing off at the 16th hole at Cypress Point, and inside the magazine, in addition to the golf piece, was an eclectic mix of stories

Brimming with Possibilities

The cover of a 1953 test issue of the as-yet-unnamed SPORTS ILLUSTRATED *featured the crowd at an Oklahoma-Nebraska football game in Lincoln.*

on hunting, fishing, snorkeling, bowling and Ping-Pong (even a piece on 15th-century jousting art) as well as baseball, motor sports and horse racing. For both dummy issues, the cover took the spectators' point of view and evoked the pleasure of watching sports.

That point of view was refined over the next 56 years. Covers were simpler in the 1950s, when America apparently had more time for hunting the chukar partridge ('55) or musing over a preview of the Yale-Dartmouth game ('56). Now there are more action photos, more words and small inset images, but the cover is still closer to a snapshot of the week than an oil painting of the era. Put them all together in a collection like this, though, and something wonderful happens: Those weeks add up to eras, and the snapshots become a panorama of the changing landscape of sport.

Being No. 1 is a recurring theme on the cover—and that's not counting the infamous 1972 issue when Walter Iooss Jr.'s photo of Miami

Dolphins running backs Jim Kiick and Larry Csonka featured Csonka surreptitiously flashing his middle finger. The editors missed it, but a riot of howling letters soon alerted them. In fact, SI receives more comments about its cover choices than about any other subject, and write-in campaigns are often mounted in complaint—most recently for the Global Warming issue in 2007.

An SI cover becomes an almost instant pop icon, though there are those who doubt whether gracing it is necessarily a good thing. Not that being on the cover 22 times has adversely affected Jack Nicklaus. Nor did Michael Jordan, who hit the cover trifecta by being photographed while playing basketball, golf and baseball, suffer from his 49 appearances. Still, the so-called SI cover jinx is part of America's sporting mindscape, the great unscripted drama, wherein strange things have happened to cover subjects with uncomfortable frequency since the early days of the magazine (page 8).

There is no greater student of SI covers than Scott Smith, who has put together a collection of autographed covers that includes, by his calculation, 93% of the nearly 3,000 SI issues published by the end of 2009. Of the 2,853 covers that have a human on them, Smith has 2,657 that are signed by at least one subject.

The relentless Smith will stop at almost nothing for a signature. In 1988 he made a trip to L.A., hunting for missing subjects. One of his stops was the hospital bed of frail and sleeping bridge expert Charles Goren, who had appeared on SI's cover in 1957, '60 and '64. Smith insists that he didn't disturb the ailing man, but he waited, magazines and Sharpie in hand, murmuring "Charles? ... Charles?" In vain, it turned out.

Smith clearly has issues. Most of them are catalogued by sport, alphabetized, placed in plastic folders and stored on shelves in his northern New Jersey home, but several thousand more unsigned copies are piled in his garage. He works in sales for a company that restructures debt, but

since receiving his first SI subscription at 13 from his grandmother, getting covers signed has been what he really does. And each week he judges the book by its cover: easy signs, hard signs.

Smith's is a Sisyphean task. As soon as he gets his latest cover signed or tracks down an autograph he has waited so long to nail, a new issue arrives in his mailbox. (No Greek mythological figure has graced the cover, but four football players from Athens, Ga., have.) Smith embraced the challenge, and his work has been made easier on occasion in the age of the Internet. He was able to buy a signed 1967 Roberto Clemente cover on eBay for $900, but he refused to pay the $750 per signature he says Mark McGwire once tried to charge him.

So it was sweet when Smith broke the 4,000-signature mark in March of 2010 after taking a trip to Florida to try to get McGwire to sign. "He's on 10 covers and for the past 15 years he's been near impossible," says Smith. "Actually one of the nastiest athletes you'd ever want to try to get a signature from. Once these 'big shots' get humbled, as he did with his steroids admission, they try to get the public on their side again by being nice. I took a flier on that fact and spent a week in Jupiter at spring training. Over four days, I was able to get him on the eight covers I needed."

Smith estimates his SI collection is worth well over a million dollars, a reminder that a picture truly can be worth more than 1,000 words ... if it is autographed by Ali, Nicklaus or even Dewey Buck, the Oklahoma trombone player who was on the cover in 1954. Smith says his obsession has never been primarily about money. "This is just a blast, seeing who's on the cover and then getting it signed."

Most readers, however, simply want to see who made the cover, and that choice can resonate—as the late Charles Goren might have said—in spades.

If we get it right. ☐

DUMMY
THE NEW WEEKLY SPORT MAGAZINE

Leadoff Hitter

The second dummy issue of SI also took the spectators' point of view—this time watching a golfer on the 16th tee at Cypress Point in Pebble Beach.

SPORTS ILLUSTRATED

NOVEMBER 18, 1957
America's National Sports Weekly
25 CENTS
$7.50 A YEAR

WHY OKLAHOMA
IS UNBEATABLE

The Jinx Factor

BY ALEXANDER WOLFF

"NO COVER!"

THE MAN BARKING THOSE WORDS ON THE END OF THE phone line was Bill Parcells, whose New England Patriots had just won the 1996 AFC title game. And here he was, placing a call to his daughter, Jill, then an employee in SI's events-marketing department, in the hope that she might sway the magazine's coverage.

What could possibly move a hugely successful and presumably rational NFL coach, with a Super Bowl appearance looming, to concern himself with whether his team would grace sundry American coffee tables for a particular week in mid-winter? A four-letter word could: the JINX.

THE 1957 SOONERS, *winners of 47 straight, were immediately hexed by the Jinx, which got its own cover in 2002 (above).*

The Jinx Is Born

SI had been in existence for just six months when slalom champion Jill Kinmont made the cover. The issue was still on the stands when she crashed into a tree and was paralyzed for life, a heartbreaking tale told in the film, The Other Side of the Mountain.

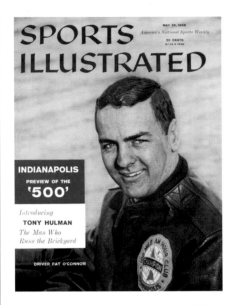

MAY 26, 1958

A Parting Smile

A week after a confidently grinning Pat O'Connor graced SI's preview of the 1958 Indianapolis 500, he was the lone casualty in a spectacular 15-car pileup on the first lap of the race, a crash which led to important safety changes in U.S. racing.

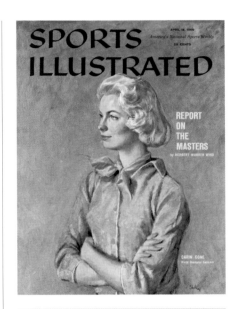

APRIL 18, 1960

Swimming Sensation Is Sunk

Carin Cone was undefeated in the 100-meter backstroke for four straight years when she was featured on SI's cover as America's best hope for gold at the 1960 Olympics. She lost her next race and a few weeks later failed to qualify for Rome.

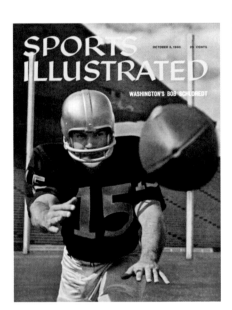

OCTOBER 3, 1960

Slipping Through His Fingers

Shown in posed action taking a shotgun snap, Washington's All-America quarterback Bob Schloredt felt the cover curse's sting a week later when his heavily favored Huskies lost to Navy 15–14, thanks to a Schloredt fumble—of a shotgun snap!

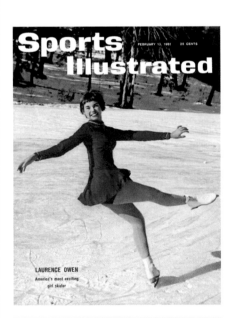

FEBRUARY 13, 1961

The Ultimate Price

Laurence Owen was just 16 when she won the U.S. figure skating championship, earning SI's cover. A week later she and the entire U.S. delegation were killed when their plane crashed en route to the world championships in Prague.

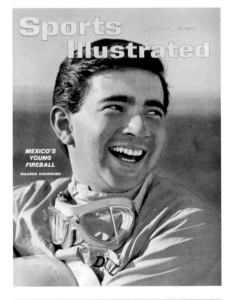

MARCH 26, 1962

Tragedy Strikes Again

Ricardo Rodriguez was a 20-year-old Formula One racing sensation from Mexico City when he was featured on SI's cover, but the billing turned out to be a particularly poor choice of words when he died in a fiery crash later that year.

The curse of the SI cover strikes man (Wilbur Wood of the Chicago White Sox, who was 13–3 when he made a 1973 cover appearance, then lost eight of his next nine decisions). It strikes woman (swimmer Carin Cone, unbeaten in the 100-meter backstroke for four years leading up to the '60 Olympic trials, failed to qualify for the Games after her cover). It hits man and woman (golfer Doug Sanders and his wife, Joan, shared a cover in January '62 and were divorced less than a year later); and man and beast. (Two months after Steve Cauthen's cover in '77, the leg of his mount, Baystreak, was broken in a three-horse pileup, and Cauthen suffered multiple fractures and required 25 stitches.)

It has afflicted athletes who have scarcely begun their careers: The Royals' Clint Hurdle, THIS YEAR'S PHENOM (1978), wasn't, and Tony Mandarich of the Packers, THE BEST OFFENSIVE LINE PROSPECT EVER ('89), was suspect from his first snap; high school pitching phenom Jon Peters, '89's SUPERKID, hurt his right arm in college and wound up as student manager at Texas A&M. The Jinx is unforgiving, and it has been that way right from the start.

IT WAS A SERIES OF FOUR CURSED COVERS in a six-year span early in the magazine's history that established the legend of the SI Jinx. In 1955, the week that an issue featuring her was on the stands, skier Jill Kinmont struck a tree during a practice run and was paralyzed from the neck down. WHY OKLAHOMA IS UNBEATABLE wasn't an insupportable cover billing, given that the Sooners in November '57 had won 47 straight games, but their 7–0 loss to Notre Dame the following Saturday made people start to notice the SI link. In '58 the magazine's Indy 500 preview featured Pat O'Connor, who was killed in a 15-car pileup during the first lap. Skater Laurence Owen appeared on the cover in '61, billed as AMERICA'S MOST EXCITING GIRL SKATER; two days after the cover date Owen and the rest of the U.S. skating team perished in a plane crash.

Since then, the Jinx has steadily, and sometimes spectacularly, struck. And the more unequivocal, braggadocious or brimming with superlative a cover image or billing is, the lower that subject seems likely to be laid. When SI told the world in 1968 that the St. Louis Cardinals' Curt Flood was BASEBALL'S BEST CENTERFIELDER, he immediately went 0 for 14 with an error before missing five games with an injury. LSU cornerback Tommy Casanova, the BEST PLAYER IN THE NATION ('71), would miss five games after pulling his hamstring in the season opener. Oregon State point guard Gary Payton, another BEST PLAYER IN THE NATION ('90), would score five points in a game that week, 22 below his average, to end a streak of 50 games in which he had scored in double figures. Ivan Ivankov of Belarus, who appeared on the cover of SI's 2000 Olympic preview in gold paint, might have been THE WORLD'S BEST GYMNAST, but he wasn't good enough to win a medal of any hue. And the Jinx answered with an emphatic No when the magazine asked of Shaq, CAN HE DELIVER A RING TO THE KING? during the 2010 NBA playoffs. The issue came out on a Tuesday and the Cavaliers lost that night to the Celtics and again two nights later, sending the would-be king, LeBron James, home in embarrassing defeat in Round 2.

Going to regional covers for the 2009 College Football Preview issue did not distract the Jinx. Oregon, Ole Miss and Oklahoma State were all touted as BCS BUSTERS, and the Jinx systematically picked them off: Oregon in Week 1, Oklahoma State in Week 2 and Ole Miss in Week 3.

But no college football team has suffered more from being on SI's cover than Nebraska. In 1972 the Cornhuskers, national champions two years running, supplied three players and coach Bob Devaney for that year's preview issue heralding the team's preseason No. 1 ranking and drive for THREE STRAIGHT—and thereby assured its 20–17 loss to unranked UCLA in the first game of the season. In 1978, it was déjà voodoo all over again. Running back Rick Berns graced the cover after a defeat of No. 1 Oklahoma, and Husker Nation looked forward to a meeting with Penn State for the national championship, a hope dashed when Nebraska lost its next game, 35–31 to Missouri. In '84 running back Jeff Smith made the cover, then missed his next game due to an ankle injury, and the top-ranked Cornhuskers lost to Syracuse. A dozen years later, right after running back Ahman Green was on the cover, he knocked the ball through his own end zone, resulting in a safety, during a 19–0 loss to Arizona State, a team that Nebraska, winner of 26 previous games, had beaten 77–28 a year earlier. So don't tell Husker fans that jinxes don't exist.

NO ONE HAS BEEN QUICKER TO pooh-pooh the Jinx than the pooh-bahs of the magazine. In the early days of SI, the editors had to send color plates to the engraver up to six weeks before publication, and that led to a number of "jinxes" that took effect before the magazine even hit the stands. The most chilling: Blue-blooded horseman Bill Woodward Jr. was to have been SI's 1955 SPORTSMAN OF THE YEAR. He had posed for the cover with his wife, Ann, his prize thoroughbred, Nashua, and Eddie Arcaro, the jockey who had ridden Nashua to victories in the Preakness and the Belmont. The weekend the cover was to print, however, Ann accidentally shot and killed her husband. SI managing editor Sid James hastily shipped to the engraver a head shot of Brooklyn Dodgers pitcher Johnny Podres. The picture was lame, and so was the choice of Podres as Sportsman of the Year. Although he had defeated the Yankees in Game 7 of the World Series, he had lost more games than he'd won that year. But Podres had the inestimable advantage of not being dead.

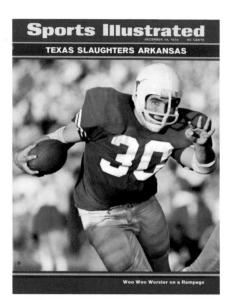

The Slaughter Rule

Texas was 10–0, winner of 30 straight games and an overwhelming title favorite when Steve Worster was featured on SI's cover. In their next game, the Longhorns fumbled nine times in a 24–11 loss to Notre Dame in the Cotton Bowl.

SEPTEMBER 11, 1972

Beginning of the End

Nebraska had won two straight national titles and was positioned for a third when coach Bob Devaney and a handful of his stars fronted SI's college football preview. The Huskers immediately lost their first game of the season, to unranked UCLA.

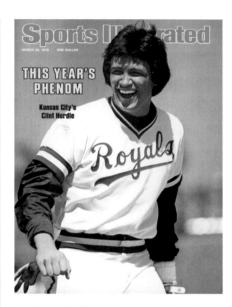

MARCH 20, 1978

Not This or Any Other Year

The Jinx seemed to take particular exception to SI's notion that the Kansas City Royals' Clint Hurdle was a player to watch. He ended up with just seven homers that season and the weight of expectations was a drag on his entire career.

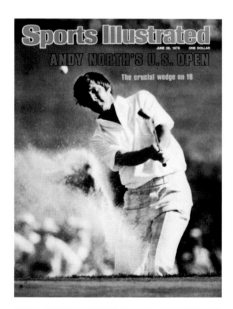

JUNE 26, 1978

North Goes South

Andy North was honored with the SI cover after winning the U.S. Open in 1978; he would not win for seven years after that. He did win a second Open title though, in 1985, and once again tempted the cover Jinx. He never won again on Tour.

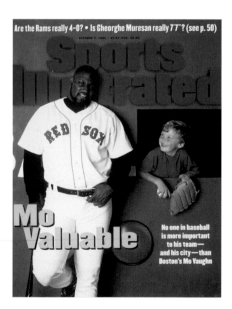

OCTOBER 2, 1995

Mo or Less

Mo Vaughn was just finishing a banner season with 39 homers and 126 RBIs when he made this appearance on the eve of the playoffs. He immediately went into a slump, going 0 for 14 as the Red Sox were swept by the Indians in three games.

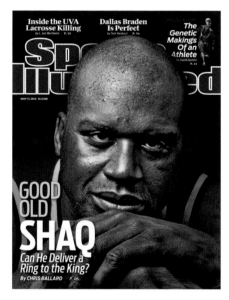

MAY 17, 2010

Shaq Attack

The Cavaliers were favorites to win it all in the 2010 playoffs when SI's cover asked if Shaquille O'Neal could help clinch a title for LeBron James. Cleveland lost to Boston the day the issue came out and again two days later, and the Cavs were out in Round 2.

Mark Mulvoy, who ran the magazine for almost 10 years during the 1980s and '90s, likes to point out that no one has graced the magazine's cover more often than Michael Jordan, Muhammad Ali, Kareem Abdul-Jabbar, Magic Johnson or Jack Nicklaus. The Fab Five have appeared on the cover of SI a total of 154 times, and the exposure hardly impeded their careers.

Former executive editor Peter Carry, who joined the magazine as an intern in 1963, has long contended that the Jinx is nothing more than what statisticians call "regression to the mean," and normal folks call "water seeking its own level." In other words when Greg Maddux of the Atlanta Braves, who hadn't lost since May '95, made the cover in August of that year, he was in the midst of a streak of 10 victories and 14 starts without a defeat, the most dazzling stretch of a fine career. Was his surrendering of five runs, eight hits and five walks in 6⅔ innings in his next start the work of the Jinx, or simply evidence of his membership in the human race?

The difficulty champs have in repeating, the so-called Cy Young Jinx, the "sophomore slump"—all are examples of regression to the mean. Fact: Among baseball players who hit .300 or better for a season, 80% hit for a lower average a year later. This isn't necessarily evidence that they've forgotten how to hit. It's more likely proof that they aren't, on balance, as good as a lofty average might have briefly suggested.

OVER TIME, ATTEMPTS HAVE BEEN made to examine the Jinx quantitatively. In 1984, two students at USC's Graduate School of Journalism, Tim Leone and Robbie Gluckson, examined a random sample of 271 covers. Team Trojan concluded that cover subjects maintained or *improved* their level of performance almost 58% of the time.

Seventeen years later, SI set out to do the definitive study. Researchers Albert Chen and Tim Smith crunched mountains of data amassed during six months of digging. Breaking out covers by sport and athlete, team and school, amateur and professional, and by kind of Jinx, they analyzed the fate of virtually all of SI's 2,456 cover subjects up to the Jan. 21, 2002 issue.

Thanks to the forensic assistance of the online database LexisNexis, as well as yellowing newspapers in libraries and the fruits of many phone calls to longtime staffers and cover subjects, they hunted down more than the statistical details to which Leone and Gluckson limited themselves. For instance if you did nothing more than check the box scores, you'd know only that Miami Hurricanes quarterback Vinny Testaverde missed a game in '86 with an injury. What you might have missed is the fact that he was injured in a motor-scooter accident six days after appearing on our cover.

To be judged an instance of the Jinx, Chen and Smith decided that a misfortune had to be measurable and relatively immediate. In other words, if SI picked, say, Florida State as its No. 1 team in August, and the Seminoles failed to bag a bid to a bowl game in December, the Jinx was off the hook. On the other hand, when the New York Islanders, in their drive for their fifth straight Stanley Cup, lost in five to the Edmonton Oilers after their cover appearance in 1984; or when the Indians—heralded on the '87 baseball preview issue with the bold prediction BELIEVE IT! CLEVELAND IS THE BEST TEAM IN THE AMERICAN LEAGUE—started 1–10 and lost 101 games that season, in each case, kudos to the Jinx.

In baseball and basketball, a hitting or shooting slump or a losing streak had to set in within two weeks of a cover appearance for the Jinx to be implicated. Thus when the Philadelphia Phillies' Mike Schmidt hit .189 over a six-week stretch following a cover appearance, a slump so bad that the club switched its All-Star third baseman to first base, the Jinx got the credit. In football the loss or lousy performance had to take place the next weekend. For Olympians the researchers compared the athlete's showing at the Games with the medal each was forecast to win. For injuries, the month following the cover turn was examined.

In the end the sleuths came up with six categories of misfortune—an individual slump; a team slump; an individual blunder or bad play; an individual injury or death; a bad loss or lousy performance by a team or individual; and a failure to win a title after having been featured during the postseason. A seventh category was added to accommodate miscellaneous calamities, like Nike's stock plunge shortly after CEO Phil Knight appeared on the cover in 1993.

The results: Of the 2,456 covers SI had run, 913 featured a person who, or a team that, suffered some verifiable misfortune that conformed to the definition—a healthy Jinx rate of 37.2%. The majority of those instances (52.7%) were bad losses or lousy performances by a team, followed by declines in individual performance, bad loss or lousy performance by an individual, postseason failure, injury or death and blunder or bad play.

Of course, it would be wise to challenge that 37.2% figure with the simple query: Compared to what? If SI didn't exist, if there had been no Jan. 23, 1984, cover for Wayne Gretzky to appear on, would the Great One have extended his scoring streak beyond 51 consecutive games, rather than watch it end on Jan. 28? Would Paul Hornung and Notre Dame have lost three straight after appearing in '56? Would the California Angels' Nolan Ryan, 10–3 when he graced the cover in '75, have dropped his next eight decisions? Would all these diminished performances have happened regardless of the magazine cover?

Well, that's what makes the Jinx a Sphinx. SI does exist—has for more than 55 years—so there's no way to simulate its absence. And anyway, a little mystery never hurts. Even Carl Sagan knew that. In *The Demon-Haunted World,* the famed rationalist observed: "What's the harm of a little mystification? It sure beats boring statistical analyses."

We'll let that be the final word. ☐

The Breakdown

The good, the bad and the most prolific: slicing and dicing the SI covers by the numbers

Michael Jordan (49)

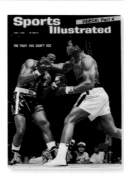

Muhammad Ali (38)

Magic Johnson (23)

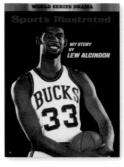

Kareem Abdul-Jabbar (22)

Jack Nicklaus (22)

The Alltime List

Ranking the athletes who have graced the cover at least four times

Michael Jordan 49	Ken Griffey Jr. 9	Tony Dorsett 6	Randy Johnson 5	Larry Csonka. 4
Muhammad Ali 38	Marvin Hagler 9	Larry Holmes. 6	Jason Kidd. 5	Mary Decker 4
Magic Johnson 23	Dan Marino 9	Evander Holyfield 6	Elle Macpherson. 5	Doug Flutie 4
Kareem Abdul-Jabbar. . 22	Willie Mays 9	Bo Jackson 6	Moses Malone. 5	Franco Harris. 4
Jack Nicklaus 22	Mark McGwire. 9	Sandy Koufax 6	Billy Martin 5	Thomas Hearns. 4
Tiger Woods 19	Joe Namath. 9	Carl Lewis 6	Phil Mickelson. 5	Gordie Howe 4
Larry Bird. 17	Bill Russell. 9	Karl Malone 6	Stan Musial 5	Ingemar Johansson 4
Shaquille O'Neal 16	O.J. Simpson 9	Jim McMahon 6	Bobby Orr. 5	Al Kaline. 4
Pete Rose. 16	Ted Williams 9	Michael Phelps 6	Walter Payton 5	Bob Knight. 4
Mike Tyson 15	Barry Bonds. 8	Gary Player 6	Scottie Pippen. 5	Mario Lemieux 4
Arnold Palmer 14	Jimmy Connors. 8	Dennis Rodman. 6	Nolan Ryan 5	Denny McLain. 4
Bill Walton 14	Roberto Duran. 8	Alex Rodriguez 6	Deion Sanders. 5	Donovan McNabb. 4
Kobe Bryant 13	Reggie Jackson. 8	Ralph Sampson. 6	Mike Schmidt 5	Albert Pujols 4
Mickey Mantle. 13	Floyd Patterson. 8	Tom Seaver 6	Michael Spinks 5	Manny Ramirez. 4
John Elway 12	Wilt Chamberlain 7	Fran Tarkenton 6	Sammy Sosa 5	Jerry Rice 4
Patrick Ewing 12	Roger Clemens 7	Tom Watson. 6	Tim Tebow 5	Brooks Robinson 4
Wayne Gretzky 12	Julius Erving 7	Steve Young. 6	Lee Trevino 5	Bart Starr. 4
Derek Jeter 12	George Foreman 7	Troy Aikman. 5	Johnny Unitas. 5	Jim Taylor 4
Sugar Ray Leonard. 12	Joe Frazier. 7	Bjorn Borg 5	Hank Aaron 4	Y.A. Tittle 4
Tom Brady 11	John McEnroe. 7	George Brett 5	Marcus Allen 4	Joe Theismann 4
Brett Favre. 11	Cal Ripken Jr. 7	Lou Brock 5	Carmelo Anthony 4	Al Unser 4
LeBron James. 11	David Robinson. 7	Reggie Bush. 5	Eddie Arcaro 4	Dwyane Wade. 4
Joe Montana. 11	Jim Ryun 7	Eric Dickerson. 5	Arthur Ashe. 4	Maury Wills. 4
Emmitt Smith. 11	Darryl Strawberry. 7	Tim Duncan 5	Rick Barry 4	Carl Yastrzemski. 4
Lance Armstrong 10	Herschel Walker 7	Dwight Gooden 5	Yogi Berra 4	Vince Young. 4
Kevin Garnett 10	Kurt Warner. 7	Tyler Hansbrough. 5	Rod Carew 4	
Sonny Liston. 10	Charles Barkley 6	John Havlicek 5	Gary Carter 4	Stats through
Peyton Manning 10	Johnny Bench. 6	Bobby Hull. 5	Steve Cauthen. 4	May 2010

MOST GLARING OMISSION

Annika Sorenstam

Winner of 72 LPGA tour events, 10 major championships, eight-time Solheim Cup team member and eight-time women's player of the year. Number of SI covers: 0

RUNNERS-UP

Cris Carter

Eight-time NFL Pro Bowl wideout, retired as No. 2 alltime leader in NFL catches (1,101) and TDs (130). Number of SI covers: 0.

Red Auerbach

Won 938 games, nine NBA championships as Celtics coach and seven more titles as team exec. Number of SI covers: 0.

The Rise of King Football

A decade-by-decade analysis of SI's covers shows the changing influence of the major sports in the U.S. While baseball has remained steady and boxing has declined badly, football now rules

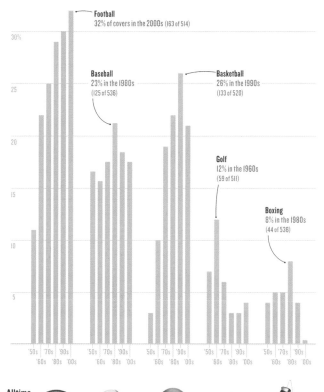

Football
32% of covers in the 2000s (163 of 514)

Baseball
23% in the 1980s
(125 of 536)

Basketball
26% in the 1990s
(133 of 520)

Golf
12% in the 1960s
(59 of 511)

Boxing
8% in the 1980s
(44 of 536)

'50s '70s '90s   '50s '70s '90s   '50s '70s '90s   '50s '70s '90s   '50s '70s '90s
 '60s '80s '00s   '60s '80s '00s   '60s '80s '00s   '60s '80s '00s   '60s '80s '00s

Alltime Cover Leaders:

Football	Baseball	Basketball	Golf	Boxing
26%	**20%**	**18%**	**6%**	**5%**
of all covers				
748 total	565	516	163	133

Gambling Coverage? You Bet

As long as there have been sports there have been wagers made on them—not always on the up-and-up—and SI has done its part to keep the games honest

Gambling in Vegas

SI examined the wows and the woes of Sin City in 1959.

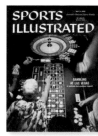

The Old Switcheroo

Amazing tale of mistaken identity and fraud in '77.

Inside a Fix

In '78 SI told how bribing jockeys led to rigged races.

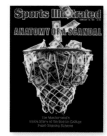

Point Shaving at BC

Fixer Henry Hill told the tale in his own words in '81.

Betting on the Web

A '98 look at a new and troubling phenomenon.

Ascent of Manning

Other fathers and sons have been on SI's cover, but no family can match the Mannings with three members who have shared that honor, a total of 13 times

September 14, 1970
Archie made the cover as All-SEC QB at Ole Miss.

December 22, 2003
Peyton is the family leader with 10 covers.

January 28, 2008
The Giants' Super Bowl run elevated Eli.

Couplings

These married pairs share a unique distinction: his and hers SI covers

Doak Walker ♥ Skeeter Werner
On covers a month apart in '55, they wed in '68.

Ray Knight ♥ Nancy Lopez
She got her cover in '78, eight years before his.

Andre Agassi ♥ Steffi Graf
Have the marital record with six—three each.

Greg Norman ♥ Chris Evert
A 15-month marriage but five lasting covers.

Nomar Garciaparra ♥ Mia Hamm
Cover Jinx got him but left their union alone.

How the Colleges Rank

Oklahoma is No. 1 with the most covers of any school in all sports combined (regional editions included)

Paul Hornung (top) had one Irish cover; Billy Sims had two for the Sooners; UCLA's Bill Walton, the most honored collegian, had eight.

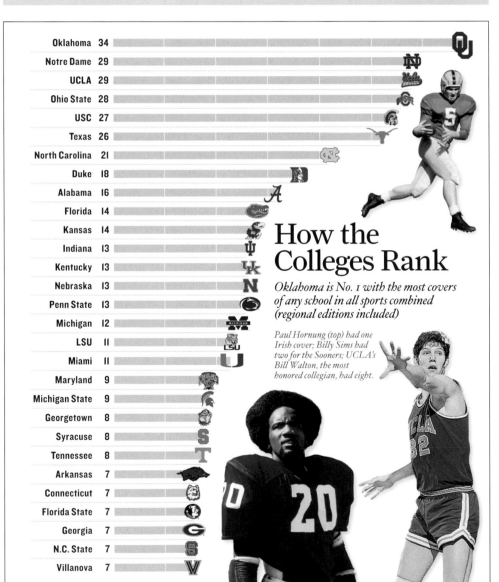

School	Covers
Oklahoma	34
Notre Dame	29
UCLA	29
Ohio State	28
USC	27
Texas	26
North Carolina	21
Duke	18
Alabama	16
Florida	14
Kansas	14
Indiana	13
Kentucky	13
Nebraska	13
Penn State	13
Michigan	12
LSU	11
Miami	11
Maryland	9
Michigan State	9
Georgetown	8
Syracuse	8
Tennessee	8
Arkansas	7
Connecticut	7
Florida State	7
Georgia	7
N.C. State	7
Villanova	7

The Decades at a Glance

There are common denominators in every era, including man's best friend

	1950s	1960s	1970s	1980s	1990s	2000s
The Team *Part of capturing the zeitgeist of any era was an appearance on SI's cover*	New York Yankees	UCLA	 Miami Dolphins	 U.S. Olympic Hockey	Chicago Bulls	 Boston Red Sox
The Stare *The game face has gone eye-to-eye with SI's readers right from the start*	Ollie Matson	Sonny Liston	George Foster	 John Hannah	Randy Johnson	Ricky Williams
The Coach *As a rule, coaches don't make hit covers, but these icons were unavoidable*	Bud Wilkinson	Vince Lombardi	Bear Bryant	 Bobby Knight	Bill Parcells	Bill Belichick
♥ The throb *From a cupid with bow to a model-marrying QB, sexy always sells*	Ann Marston	Peggy Fleming	Joe Namath	Mary Decker	Brandi Chastain	Tom Brady
The Dogs *Canines have been a loyal standby when the need for an offbeat cover arises*	Great Dane	Bedlington Terrier	English Sheepdog	Pit Bulls	UGA V	Michael Vick's Dogs

Where There's Smoke . . .

There's usually someone celebrating a victory or themselves with a cigar. Or, in Marge Schott's case, someone with an utter disregard for convention.

Howard Cosell
Cosell appeared with his trademark stogie in 1983.

Magic Johnson
How better to portray a budding tycoon in 1990?

Michael Jordan
MJ celebrated his first repeat title in 1992.

Marge Schott
SI took an unvarnished look at Marge in 1996.

Mike Ditka
Ditka was a Saint in '98, but he still had his vices.

Cover to Cover

Mickey Mantle

1956 **1995**

At 39 years, the Mick has the longest span of covers

Gordie Howe

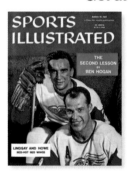 

1957 **1980**

Mr. Hockey had the greatest run as an active player

Sport	Count
Horse Racing	44
Skiing	34
Auto Racing	32
Swimming	18
Sailing	13
Soccer	13
Fishing	11
Hunting	11
Cycling	10
Figure Skating	9
Speedskating	9
Diving	5
Dog Shows	5
Gymnastics	4
Pole Vault	4
Shot Put	4
Surfing	4
Yachting	4
Bridge	3
Physical Fitness	3
Archery	2
Ballooning	2
Crew	2
High Jump	2
Javelin	2
Mountain Climbing	2
Parachuting	2
Skydiving	2
Softball	2
Snowboarding	2
Waterskiing	2
Wrestling	2
Badminton	1
Bobsledding	1
Bowling	1
Bullfighting	1
Chess	1
Equestrian	1
Fencing	1
Hydroplane Racing	1
Ice Climbing	1
Lacrosse	1
Long Jump	1
Power Boating	1
Rafting	1
Rock Climbing	1
Squash	1
Ultimate Fighting	1
Water Sports	1
Weightlifting	1

ALL SI COVERS 75% / **Other sports** 25%

Football, baseball, basketball, golf and boxing

No Sport Left Behind

Football has had 748 SI covers, hockey 74. But here's a sampling of less popular pastimes that have shone on at least one issue

Shaun White (top), Michelle Kwan and Affirmed have all had their moment on a cover.

What Were We Thinking?

When you do almost 3,000 covers, there are bound to be a few clunkers in there. Here are a few for which the editors might like to have a do-over

Danny Lopez
A bit over-the-top for a guy who fought out of L.A.

George Steinbrenner
The Boss as Napoleon: The surprise was that he said yes.

Dennis Rodman
Unclear which rare bird had more exotic plumage.

McGwire & Sosa
Classic Greek heroes? What say the chorus now?

Charles Barkley
It was the editors who could've used restraint.

Most Appearances by Team

A pair of consistent, longtime winners, the New York Yankees and Los Angeles Lakers, lead the way

New York Yankees..............70	New York Knicks.................23	Cleveland Browns..............16	Milwaukee Bucks 11	Connecticut (basketball)....5
Los Angeles Lakers.............64	Oakland Athletics 23	San Antonio Spurs.............16	New Orleans Saints............11	Denver Nuggets...................5
Dallas Cowboys 46	Philadelphia Phillies............23	Indianapolis Colts...............15	New York Rangers...............11	Michigan State (basketball) 5
Boston Red Sox 45	San Francisco Giants..........23	Nebraska (football)..............15	Portland Trail Blazers 11	Orlando Magic......................5
Chicago Bulls 44	Chicago White Sox..............22	Seattle Mariners.................15	Anaheim Angels...................10	Tennessee (football) 5
Boston Celtics.....................42	Detroit Tigers 22	Alabama (football)..............14	Chicago Blackhawks...........10	Tennessee Titans 5
Los Angeles Dodgers..........40	Ohio State (football) 22	Baltimore Colts 13	Florida (football)..................10	Arizona Diamondbacks.......4
Pittsburgh Steelers 37	Texas (football).....................22	Indiana (basketball)............13	Kansas (basketball) 10	Baltimore Ravens 4
St. Louis Cardinals...............37	Chicago Cubs 21	Kansas City Royals..............13	Kansas City Chiefs..............10	Marquette (basketball).......4
Cincinnati Reds....................36	New England Patriots 21	Kentucky (basketball) 13	San Diego Padres 10	Michigan (basketball).........4
San Francisco 49ers............33	New York Giants 21	Miami (football)...................13	Tampa Bay Buccaneers......10	Minnesota Timberwolves...4
Green Bay Packers..............31	USC (football)......................21	Philadelphia Eagles.............13	Cincinnati Bengals 8	Ohio State (basketball).......4
New York Mets.....................31	Washington Redskins..........21	Penn State (football) 13	Michigan (football)...............8	Pittsburgh Penguins 4
Oklahoma (football) 29	Atlanta Braves 20	Boston Bruins 12	Milwaukee Braves 8	Syracuse (basketball).........4
Notre Dame (football)..........27	Denver Broncos 19	Cleveland Indians 12	New Jersey Nets 8	Washington Wizards...........4
Baltimore Orioles.................26	Minnesota Twins 19	Los Angeles Rams..............12	St. Louis Rams.....................8	Arizona (basketball)............3
Miami Dolphins....................25	New York Jets......................19	Montreal Canadiens............12	Florida State (football) 7	Carolina Panthers 3
Oakland Raiders 24	Pittsburgh Pirates 19	Buffalo Bills 11	Georgia (football) 7	Villanova (basketball)..........3
UCLA (basketball)...............24	Duke (basketball)................18	Cleveland Cavaliers.............11	Maryland (basketball) 7	
Chicago Bears.....................23	North Carolina (basketball) .18	Detroit Pistons....................11	Phoenix Suns 7	Stats through
Minnesota Vikings...............23	Philadelphia 76ers 17	Houston Rockets................11	Miami Heat 6	May 2010

Same Face, Different Uniform

Michael Jordan didn't move around that much in his career, but he still appeared on SI's cover in five team uniforms, a record later tied by Shaquille O'Neal

North Carolina
Number 23 made his first cover appearance in 1983.

Chicago Bulls
Jordan was a Bull for 41 of his record 49 SI covers.

U.S. Olympic Team
The '92 Dream Team put Jordan in terrific company.

Birmingham Barons
SI covered an unsuccessful fling with baseball in '94.

Washington Wizards
Jordan's last cover came in 2003 with the Wizards.

Tackling the Tough Issues

SI has never shied from examining the things that are wrong with sports

1965
1970
1975
1980
1985
1990
1995
2000
2005
2010

The Black Athlete
A groundbreaking three-part series

Pollution
An early warning on global warming

Too Fast Too Soon
A hard look at child-racing safety

Athletes And Drugs
Was ahead of the game on steroids

Cocaine In the NFL
A shocking revelation in '82

Your Sneakers Or Your Life
Dying for a pair of Air Jordans

Monica Seles
Examining a near-fatal stabbing

Kentucky's Shame
Player payments, academic fraud

Where's Daddy?
Exposing the shame of athlete paternity

Steroids In Baseball
Ken Caminiti's stunning confession

Global Warming
Climate change's effect on sports

Pedophile Coaches
A clarion call to all parents of athletes

Celeb Sights

Not all of the stars who've been on SI's cover have been athletes

Ed Sullivan
Lining up a putt ('59)

Bob Hope
Tribe co-owner ('63)

Shirley MacLaine
Pigskin film flop ('64)

Steve McQueen
Dirt-bike racer ('71)

***Semi-Tough* cast**
Pigskin film hit ('77)

Arnold Schwarzenegger
Smokin' film star ('87)

Chris Rock
Saluted fans (2000)

Stephen Colbert
A good skate ('09)

Hail To the Chiefs

SI has its own First Family of cover subjects with four Presidents who have appeared there, including the Gipper, Ronald Reagan, who made it twice

John F. Kennedy, 1960
JFK, with Jackie, just a month after his election.

Gerald Ford, 1974
The best athlete, he was a star center at Michigan.

Ronald Reagan, 1984
Hoyas John Thompson & Pat Ewing flanked the Prez.

Ronald Reagan, 1987
Gipper & America's Cup skipper, Dennis Conner.

Bill Clinton, 1994
Most undignified Presidential billing ever.

1994
Two of the models, Kathy Ireland and Rachel Hunter, were pregnant for this shoot.

2006
Most models on the cover at once—eight.

1997
Tyra Banks's second cover appearance and first solo effort. She was the first African-American SI cover model.

2001
This photo at a Tunisian oasis is only the second cover that was shot nowhere near the ocean. The first was in Scottsdale, Ariz., in 1967.

1988
Elle Macpherson's third-straight cover. She has five cover appearances, the most of any model.

PICTURE PERFECT
Each dot shows the location of a Swimsuit Issue cover shoot.

1978
The issue that generated the most letters to the editor ever—2,947—most concerning a photo of a fishnetted Cheryl Tiegs.

1985
Paulina Porizkova, who married Ric Ocasek, is one of four cover models who wed musicians. The others: Rachel Hunter was married to Rod Stewart, Christie Brinkley to Billy Joel and Beyoncé wed Jay-Z.

TOP SELLER
1989
The 25th anniversary Swimsuit Issue, featuring Kathy Ireland in Baja, Mexico, remains the top-selling issue of SI ever.

1964
The first Swimsuit Issue: Babette March on the beach in Cozumel, Mexico.

5.1 million copies sold

WHAT WERE THEY WEARING?
How the 65 cover models were clad.

16 one-piece

35 bikinis

12 half a bikini

2009

Nothing (but paint)

2

1982

2004

SWIMSUIT:
The Facts and, Oh, the Figures

Everything you ever wanted to know about the SI Swimsuit Issue but were just too distracted to ask. The world map *(top)* shows the locale of every cover shoot, with the Caribbean leading the way. Throughout are fun facts about the annual February issue that grew from a modest beginning in 1964 into an internationally recognized institution today

WHO'S WATCHING?
Total audience for Brooklyn Decker's first cover.

21 million
2008–09 NBA total attendance

67 million
2010 Swimsuit Issue*

41 million
U.S. audience for 2010 Academy Awards

2010

* includes sales and pass-along readership

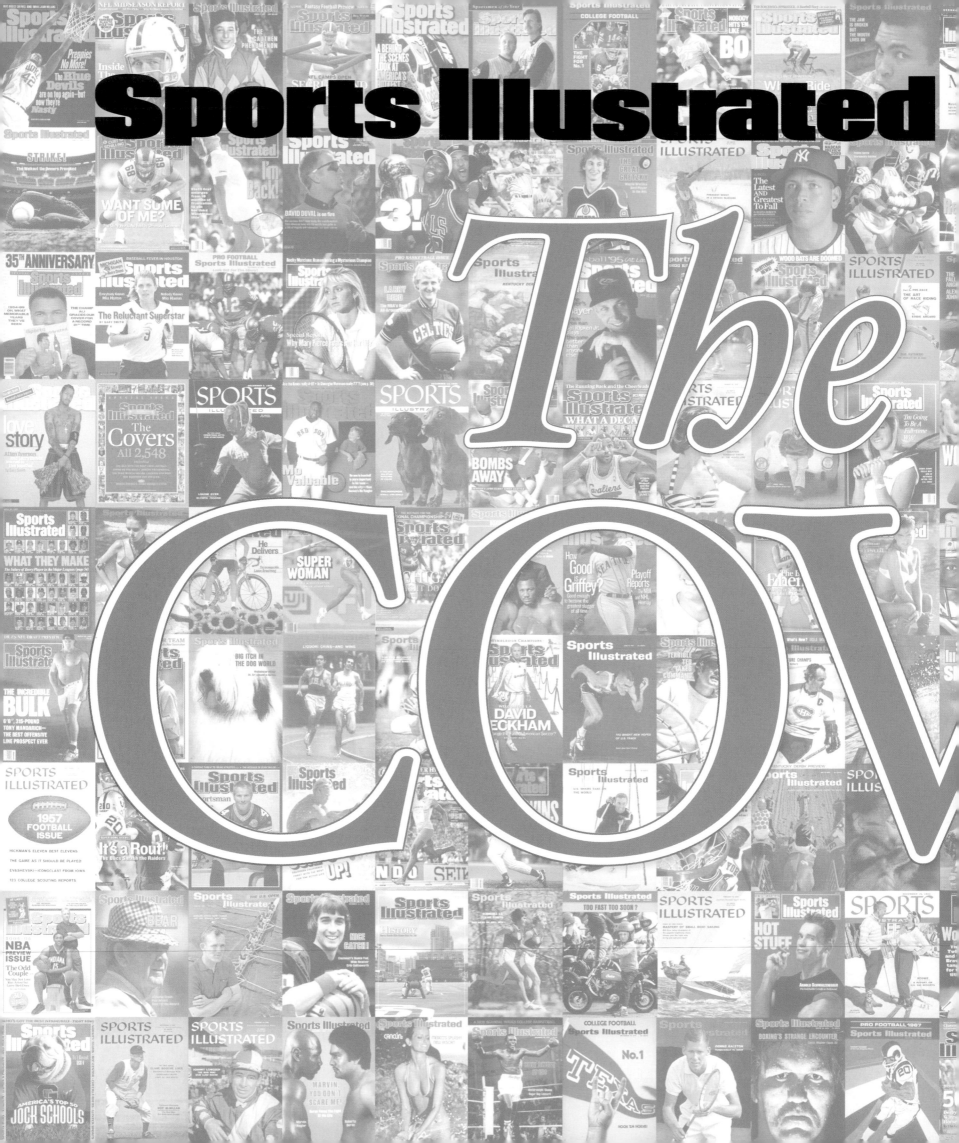

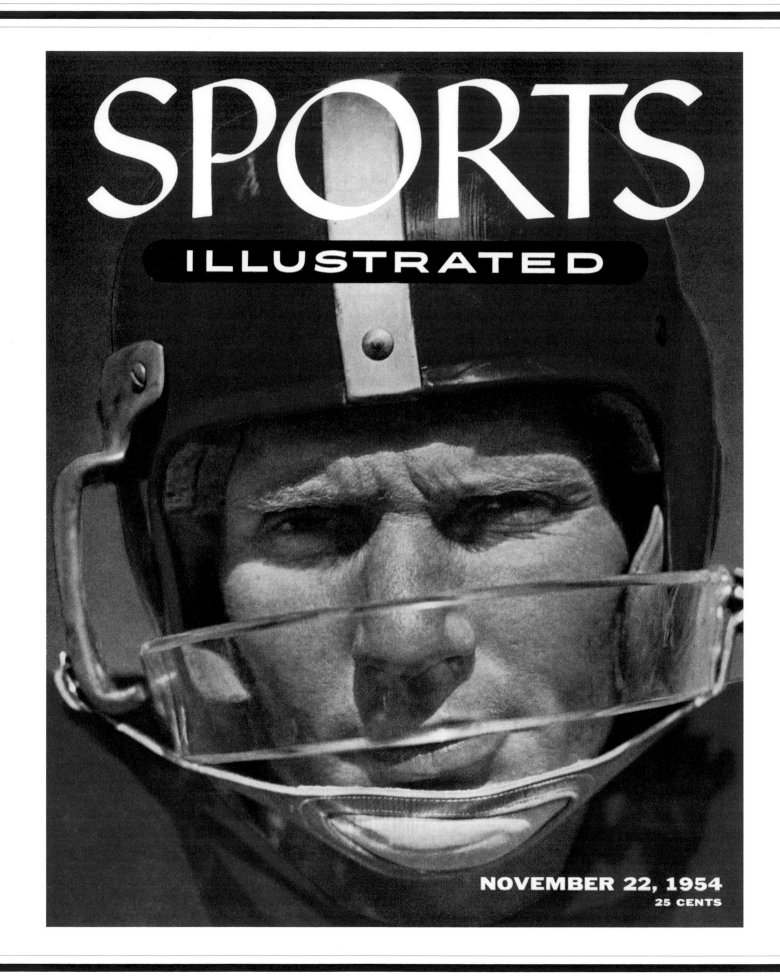

SPORTS
ILLUSTRATED

NOVEMBER 22, 1954
25 CENTS

1950–1959

Chaos and Collegiality

BY WALTER BINGHAM

FOR THE FIRST COVER OF SPORTS ILLUSTRATED, managing editor Sid James chose baseball and hit a home run. If you were launching a weekly magazine devoted to sports, what better subject to appear on the inaugural issue than the national pastime? But then, on successive covers, there appeared a cluster of golf bags, a woman wading in the Atlantic surf and a yachtsman sailing an oceangoing sloop—all geared more to what one could *do* rather than watch. And pretty soon, that was the reputation SPORTS ILLUSTRATED cultivated. It was a magazine for people who looked upon sports in an amused way, but without passion.

The business of starting any new magazine involves some trial and error, and there was no template for a weekly devoted to sports. It didn't help that James and his top aides, recruits from other Time Inc. magazines, knew next to nothing about their subject. To them, fly-fishing was as important as pro football.

The early staff was small, fewer than 50, and the feel of the place was almost like a college newspaper. The mood every Monday afternoon when an issue closed was festive and generally called for a celebration known as a pouring, essentially a cocktail party held in the art department, refreshments provided by management. Every issue was like a newborn child.

But look inside that first issue and there are some noticeable defects. The cover shot of Milwaukee slugger Eddie Mathews at bat against a backdrop of a packed County Stadium is an enduring one, but there's no story about Mathews or the Braves in the issue. There is a classic account by Paul O'Neil of a race between Roger Bannister and John Landy, the first sub-four-minute milers, and a superb piece by Gerald Holland declaring that *The Golden Age Of Sport Is Now*. At the other end of the spectrum, there was advice on how to care for a new puppy.

There were brief columns by noted writers—Grantland Rice, Red Smith, Budd Schulberg—intermingled with baseball bubble gum cards, beavers building a dam and instructions on how to get your hunting dog in shape. James had the kind of unbridled enthusiasm necessary for the editor of a startup, but he rarely encountered a story idea he didn't like.

The technological constraints of the time didn't help. It took six weeks for a cover to be shot, plated and published. It was impossible to photograph a weekend's sporting event and have it on the newsstands just days later. Put quarterback Y.A. Tittle on the cover, which SI did in November that first year, and hold your breath. The week the issue appeared, Tittle's San Francisco 49ers lost 48–7.

That sort of problem continued through the end of the decade. In late 1957, with the Cincinnati Reds apparently set to win the National League pennant, the editors decided to put shortstop Roy McMillan on the cover. Alas, the Reds folded. The magazine was stuck, but at least it could still alter the type. When readers got their issue, the Yankees and Braves were just about set for the World Series, and there was the shortstop for the second-place Reds on the front, with the billing, THE BEST WAS NOT QUITE GOOD ENOUGH.

The final cover of the '50s reveals a magazine still trying to find its identity. It showed a simulated Christmas gift, complete with ribbon and a cornucopia of offerings: a photo of a Babe Ruth paycheck, Charles Goren on bridge, a young woman in a spa, the Silver Anniversary football team, bowl game predictions, a rodeo and photos of Rome by night.

Just as uncertain was the magazine's future. By decade's end, it was still losing money. Heaps of it. The story—probably apocryphal—was that the Time Inc. board of directors voted 19–1 to fold the magazine, but the one vote against came from Henry Luce, the company's founder, and he had a visionary's certainty that it would succeed.

WALTER BINGHAM *joined SI as an edit assistant in 1955, retired as an assistant managing editor in '88 and is still a contributor.*

1954–1959

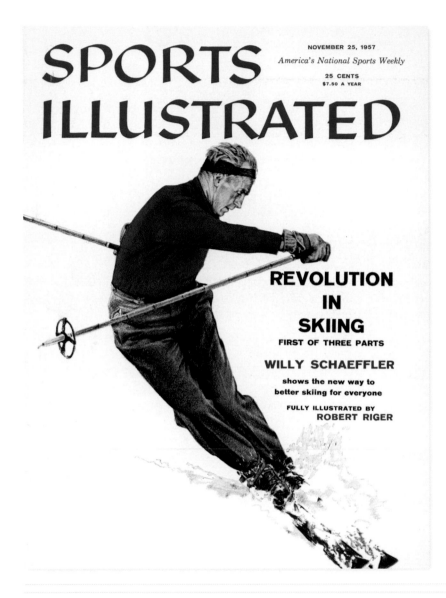

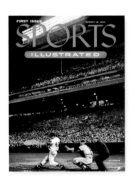

EDDIE MATHEWS
August 16, 1954

U.S. AMATEUR PREVIEW
August 23, 1954

PAMELA NELSON
August 30, 1954

YACHT RACING
September 6, 1954

AUTO RACING
September 13, 1954

CALGARY STAMPEDE
September 20, 1954

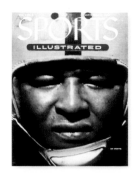

CALVIN JONES
September 27, 1954

JOYCE SELLERS
October 4, 1954

OKLAHOMA FOOTBALL
October 11, 1954

> **WE CANNOT PROMISE**
> *what victories we will*
> *report—sport is too*
> *unpredictable for that. But*
> *we do promise to bring*
> *the best of sport, all in one*
> *place—and to bring it to you*
> *with an eye for action, a nose*
> *for news and an ear for truth.*
> *And, we might add, with*
> *heart and humor.*
>
> —Henry Luce, *1959*

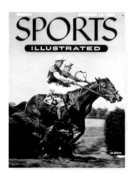

BELMONT RACING
October 18. 1954

HUNTING
October 25, 1954

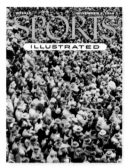

OKLAHOMA FOOTBALL
November 1, 1954

MONTAUK FISHING
November 8, 1954

DUCKS
November 15, 1954

Y.A. TITTLE
November 22, 1954

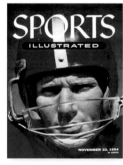

CAR RALLY
November 29, 1954

AFRICAN SAFARI
December 6, 1954

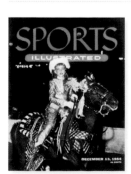

K.C. HORSE SHOW
December 13, 1954

KEN SEARS
December 20, 1954

SWISS SKIING
December 27, 1954

ROGER BANNISTER
January 3, 1955

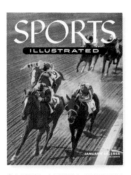

SANTA ANITA DERBY
January 10, 1955

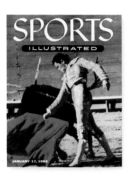

BULLFIGHTING
January 17, 1955

GYMNASTICS
January 24, 1955

JILL KINMONT
January 31, 1955

CAROL HEISS
February 7, 1955

WESTMINSTER DOGS
February 14, 1955

BETTY DI BUGNANO
February 21, 1955

RACING AT HIALEAH
February 28, 1955

BADMINTON
March 7, 1955

BUDDY WERNER
March 14, 1955

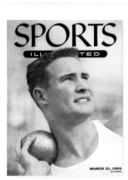

PARRY O'BRIEN
March 21, 1955

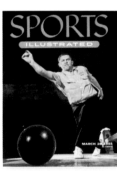

STEVE NAGY
March 28, 1955

BEN HOGAN
April 4, 1955

MAYS & DUROCHERS
April 11, 1955

AL ROSEN
April 18, 1955

TENZIG NORGAY
April 25, 1955

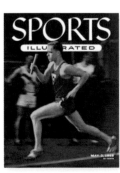

PENN RELAYS
May 2, 1955

BALLOONING
May 9, 1955

BIRD WATCHING
May 16, 1955

ZALE PERRY
May 23, 1955

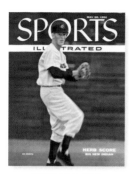

HERB SCORE
May 30, 1955

TROUT FISHING
June 6, 1955

YACHTING
June 13, 1955

ED FURGOL
June 20, 1955

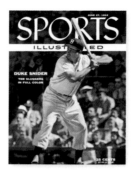

DUKE SNIDER
June 27, 1955

BULLDOGS
July 4, 1955

YOGI BERRA
July 11, 1955

SWAPS
July 18, 1955

ALPINE VACATION
July 25, 1955

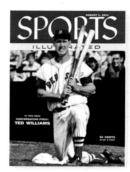

TED WILLIAMS
August 1, 1955

ANN MARSTON
August 8, 1955

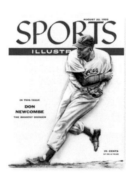

FIRST ANNIVERSARY
August 15, 1955

DON NEWCOMBE
August 22, 1955

TONY TRABERT
August 29, 1955

FRED & ART PINDER
September 5, 1955

BUD WILKINSON
September 12, 1955

ROCKY MARCIANO
September 19, 1955

WALTER ALSTON
September 26, 1955

DOAK WALKER
October 3, 1955

BIRD HUNTING
October 10, 1955

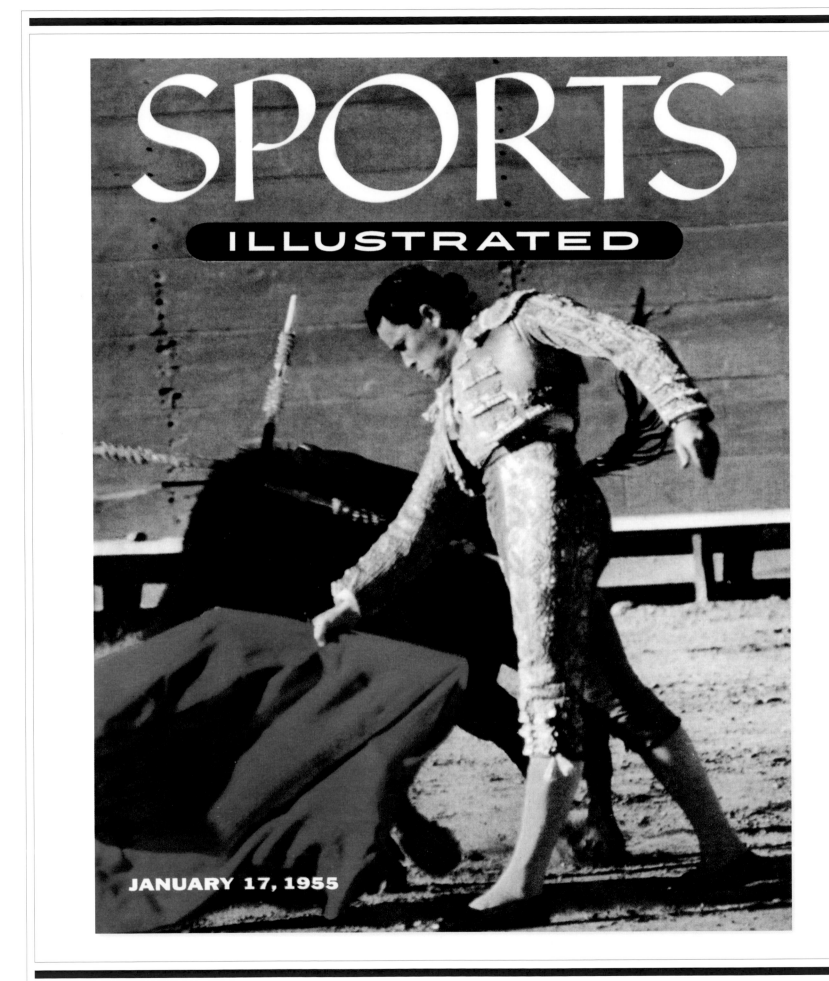

JANUARY 17, 1955

PRINCETON FOOTBALL
October 17, 1955

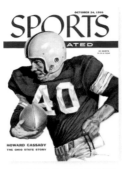

HOWARD CASSADY
October 24, 1955

PAMELA PHILLIPS
October 31, 1955

BOB PELLEGRINI
November 7, 1955

ERNEST BURTON
November 14, 1955

SKEETER WERNER
November 21, 1955

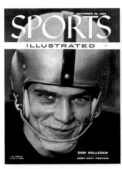

DON HOLLEDER
November 28, 1955

LOUISE DYER
December 5, 1955

DOG BREEDING
December 12, 1955

SKIING IN THE U.S.
December 19, 1955

JIM SWINK
December 26, 1955

JOHNNY PODRES
January 2, 1956

BOB COUSY
January 9, 1956

MIKE SOUCHAK
January 16, 1956

JEAN BELIVEAU
January 23, 1956

JENKINS & ALBRIGHT
January 30, 1956

RALPH MILLER
February 6, 1956

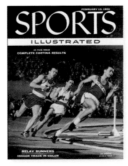

INDOOR TRACK
February 13, 1956

EVERGLADES BIRDS
February 20, 1956

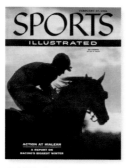

RACING AT HIALEAH
February 27, 1956

SPRING TRAINING
March 5, 1956

CHAMPION AFGHAN
March 12, 1956

ALFRED GLASSELL JR.
March 19, 1956

JIM KIMBERLY
March 26, 1956

AL WIGGINS
April 2, 1956

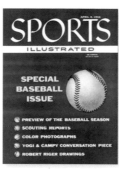

BASEBALL PREVIEW
April 9, 1956

BARBARA ROMACK
April 16, 1956

BILLY MARTIN
April 23, 1956

FLY FISHING
April 30, 1956

DERBY PREVIEW
May 7, 1956

KALINE & KUENN
May 14, 1956

JOHN LANDY
May 21, 1956

BOB SWEIKERT
May 28, 1956

FLOYD PATTERSON
June 4, 1956

SAM SNEAD
June 11, 1956

MICKEY MANTLE
June 18, 1956

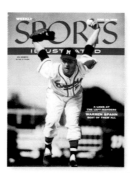

WARREN SPAHN
June 25, 1956

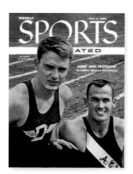

SIME & MORROW
July 2, 1956

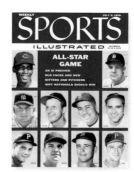

ALL-STAR GAME
July 9, 1956

CINCINNATI REDS
July 16, 1956

ADIOS HARRY
July 23, 1956

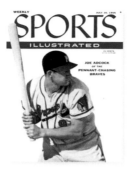

JOE ADCOCK
July 30, 1956

JEANNE STUNYO
August 6, 1956

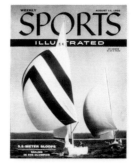

OLYMPIC SAILING
August 13, 1956

SECOND ANNIVERSARY
August 20, 1956

DORIS & RUTH GISSY
August 27, 1956

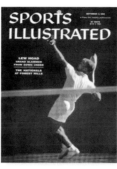

LEW HOAD
September 3, 1956

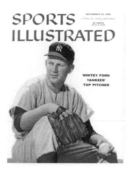

WHITEY FORD
September 10, 1956

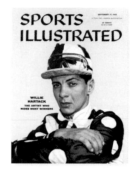

WILLIE HARTACK
September 17, 1956

FOOTBALL PREVIEW
September 24, 1956

MICKEY MANTLE
October 1, 1956

BROWN & RATTERMAN
October 8, 1956

HAROLD VANDERBILT
October 15, 1956

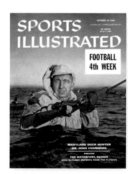

DR. JOHN CHAMBERS
October 22, 1956

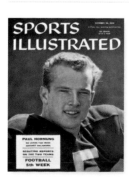

PAUL HORNUNG
October 29, 1956

YALE FOOTBALL
November 5, 1956

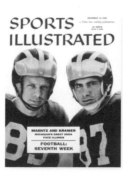

MAENTZ & KRAMER
November 12, 1956

OLYMPIC PREVIEW
November 19, 1956

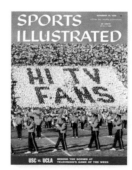

USC FOOTBALL
November 26, 1956

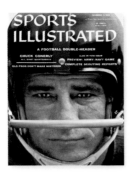

CHUCK CONERLY
December 3, 1956

OLYMPIC REVIEW
December 10, 1956

ELIZABETH GUEST
December 17, 1956

YEAR IN REVIEW
December 24, 1956

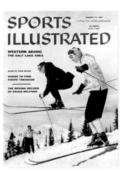

BOBBY MORROW
January 7, 1957

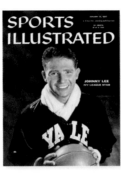

SKIING IN UTAH
January 14, 1957

JOHNNY LEE
January 21, 1957

BOSTON BRUINS
January 28, 1957

HUGH SHADELEE
February 4, 1957

WESTMINSTER DOGS
February 11, 1957

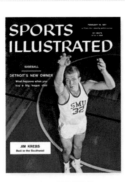

JIM KREBS
February 18, 1957

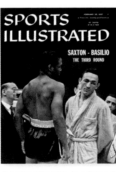

SAXTON VS. BASILIO
February 25, 1957

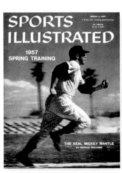

MICKEY MANTLE
March 4, 1957

BEN HOGAN
March 11, 1957

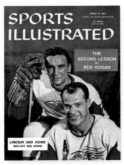

LINDSAY & HOWE
March 18, 1957

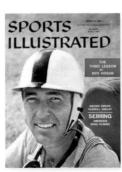

CARROLL SHELBY
March 25, 1957

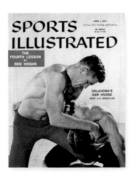

DAN HODGE
April 1, 1957

A. WELLS PECK
April 8, 1957

BASEBALL PREVIEW
April 15, 1957

SPORTS ILLUSTRATED

MARCH 3, 1958
America's National Sports Weekly

25 CENTS
$7.50 A YEAR

1958
SPRING TRAINING
ARE THE BRAVES
ON TOP TO STAY?

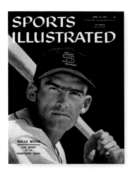
WALLY MOON
April 22, 1957

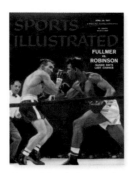
FULLMER VS. ROBINSON
April 29, 1957

DERBY PREVIEW
May 6, 1957

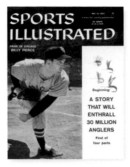
BILLY PIERCE
May 13, 1957

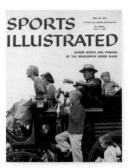
GUSSIE BUSCH
May 20, 1957

INDY 500 PREVIEW
May 27, 1957

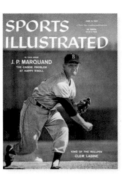
CLEM LABINE
June 3, 1957

CARY MIDDLECOFF
June 10, 1957

EDDIE ARCARO
June 13, 1957

BOB GUTOWSKI
June 20, 1957

YACHTING
July 1, 1957

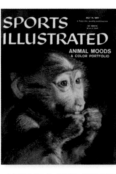
ALL-STAR GAME
July 8, 1957

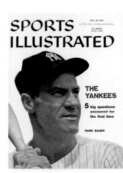
ANIMAL BEHAVIOR
July 15, 1957

HANK BAUER
July 22, 1957

FLOYD PATTERSON
July 29, 1957

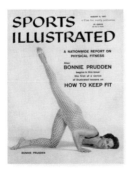
BONNIE PRUDDEN
August 5, 1957

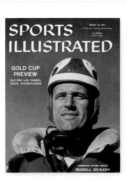
RUSSELL SCHLEEH
August 12, 1957

HICKORY SMOKE & SIMPSON
August 19, 1957

ADRIATIC BEACHES
August 26, 1957

ALTHEA GIBSON
September 2, 1957

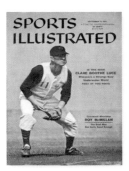

ROY McMILLAN
September 9, 1957

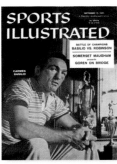

CARMEN BASILIO
September 16, 1957

COLLEGE FOOTBALL
September 23, 1957

WORLD SERIES
September 30, 1957

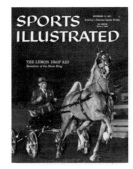

OLLIE MATSON
October 7, 1957

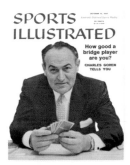

CHARLES GOREN
October 14, 1957

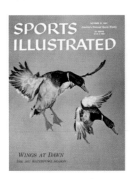

HUNTING
October 21, 1957

NATURE WALKS
October 28, 1957

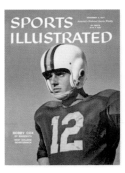

BOBBY COX
November 4, 1957

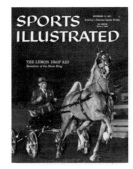

LEMON DROP KID
November 11, 1957

OKLAHOMA FOOTBALL
November 18, 1957

WILLY SCHAEFFLER
November 25, 1957

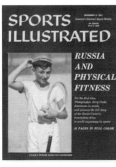

FITNESS IN RUSSIA
December 2, 1957

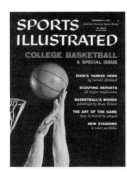

COLLEGE BASKETBALL
December 9, 1957

AMY BAIRD
December 16, 1957

YEAR IN REVIEW
December 23, 1957

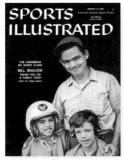

VACATION SPOTS
January 6, 1958

RECREATIONAL FLYING
January 13, 1958

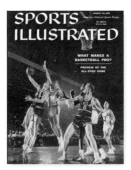

PRO BASKETBALL
January 20, 1958

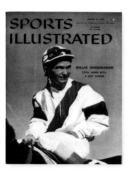

WILLIE SHOEMAKER
January 27, 1958

ELEPHANT SEALS
February 3, 1958

SALAUN & MATEER
February 10, 1958

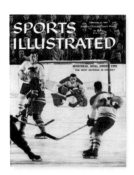

JACQUES PLANTE
February 17, 1958

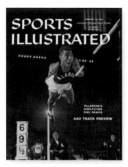

PHIL REAVIS
February 24, 1958

SPRING TRAINING
March 3, 1958

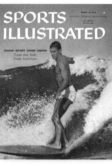

AUSTRALIAN SURFING
March 10, 1958

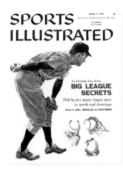

SAL MAGLIE
March 17, 1958

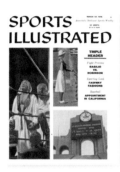

CARMEN BASILIO
March 24, 1958

ROY SIEVERS
March 31, 1958

GOLF & FISHING
April 7, 1958

BASEBALL PREVIEW
April 14, 1958

DEL CRANDALL
April 21, 1958

SILKY SULLIVAN
April 28, 1958

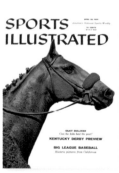

GIL McDOUGALD
May 5, 1958

AMERICA'S CUP
May 12, 1957

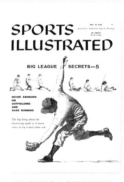

RICHIE ASHBURN
May 19, 1958

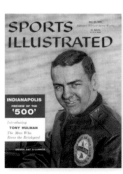

PAT O'CONNOR
May 26, 1958

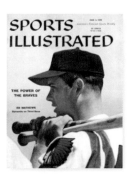

EDDIE MATHEWS
June 2, 1958

DICK MAYER
June 9, 1958

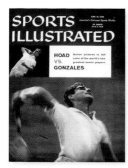

HOAD VS. GONZALES
June 16, 1958

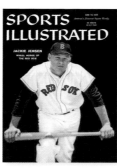

JACKIE JENSEN
June 23, 1958

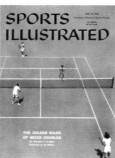

MIXED DOUBLES
June 30, 1958

ALL-STAR GAME
July 7, 1958

DOG TRAINING
July 14, 1958

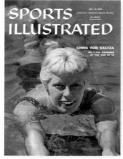

CHRIS VON SALTZA
July 21, 1958

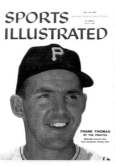

FRANK THOMAS
July 28, 1958

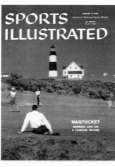

NANTUCKET GOLF
August 4, 1958

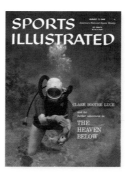

CLARE BOOTHE LUCE
August 11, 1958

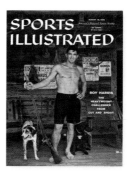

ROY HARRIS
August 18, 1958

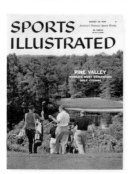

GOLF AT PINE VALLEY
August 25, 1958

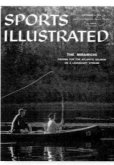

PATTERSON VS. HARRIS
September 1, 1958

SALMON FISHING
September 8, 1958

AMERICA'S CUP
September 15, 1958

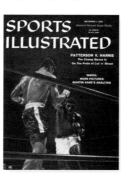

COLLEGE FOOTBALL
September 22, 1958

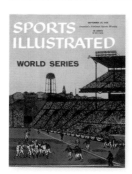

WORLD SERIES
September 29, 1958

OUTER BANKS
October 6, 1958

OHIO STATE FOOTBALL
October 13, 1958

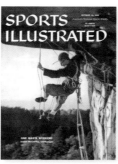

JAMES McCARTHY
October 20, 1958

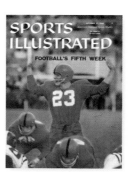

CHICK ZIMMERMAN
Octoboer 27, 1958

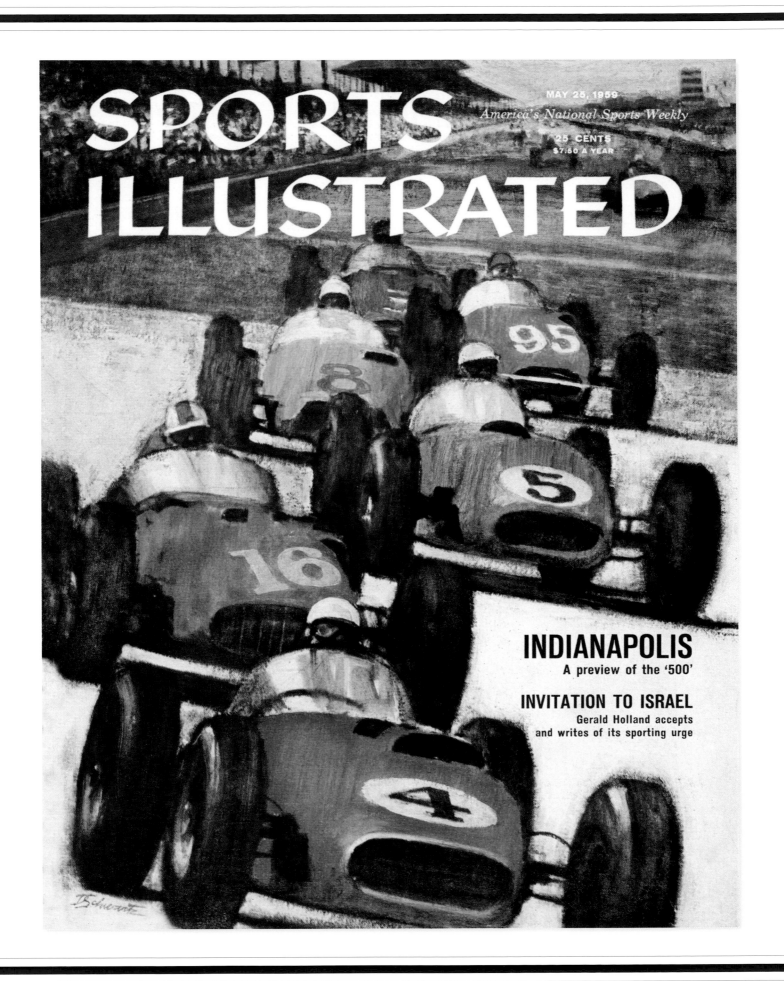

SPORTS ILLUSTRATED

MAY 25, 1959
America's National Sports Weekly

25 CENTS
$7.50 A YEAR

INDIANAPOLIS
A preview of the '500'

INVITATION TO ISRAEL
Gerald Holland accepts
and writes of its sporting urge

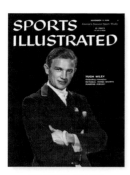

HUGH WILEY
November 3, 1958

HERB ELLIOTT
November 10, 1958

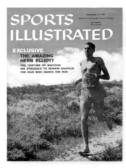

MR. & MRS. JOHN OLIN
November 17, 1958

ARMY VS. NAVY
November 24, 1958

PAT SAVIERS
December 1, 1958

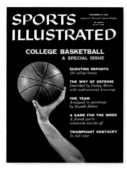

COLLEGE BASKETBALL
December 8, 1958

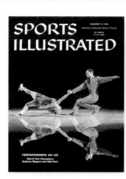

WAGNER & PAUL
December 15, 1958

YEAR IN REVIEW
December 22, 1958

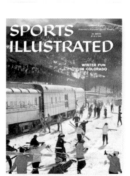

RAFER JOHNSON
January 5, 1959

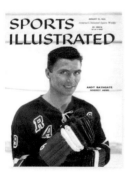

ANDY BATHGATE
January 12, 1959

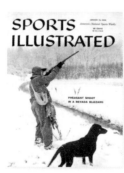

PHEASANT HUNTING
January 19, 1959

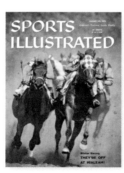

RACING AT HIALEAH
January 26, 1959

RON DELANY
February 2, 1959

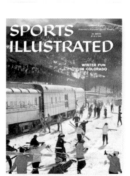

COLORADO SKIING
February 9, 1959

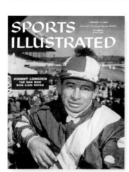

JOHNNY LONGDEN
February 16, 1959

BILL COX
February 23, 1959

CASEY STENGEL
March 2, 1959

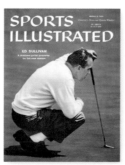

ED SULLIVAN
March 9, 1959

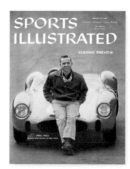

PHIL HILL
March 16, 1959

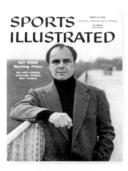

ALI KHAN
March 23, 1959

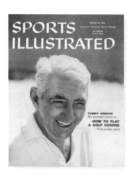

TOMMY ARMOUR
March 30, 1959

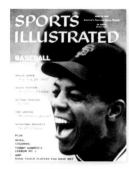

BOBBY JONES
April 6, 1959

WILLIE MAYS
April 13, 1959

BILLY TALBERT
April 20, 1959

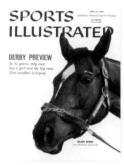

DERBY PREVIEW
April 27, 1959

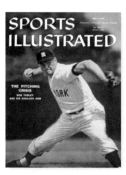

BOB TURLEY
May 4, 1959

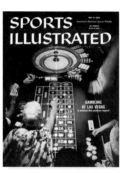

GAMBLING IN VEGAS
May 11, 1959

SAILING MOSBACHERS
May 18, 1959

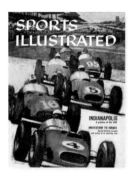

INDY 500 PREVIEW
May 25, 1959

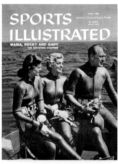

GARY COOPER
June 1, 1959

U.S. OPEN PREVIEW
June 8, 1959

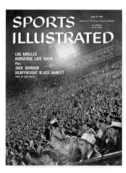

NIGHT BASEBALL
June 15, 1959

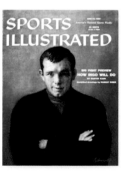

INGEMAR JOHANSSON
June 22, 1959

BIRD WATCHING
June 29, 1959

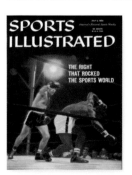

JOHANSSON–PATTERSON
July 6, 1959

BETSY COLLINS
July 13, 1959

VASILY KUZNETSOV
July 20, 1959

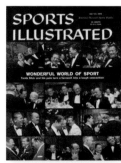

TOOTS SHOR & PALS
July 27, 1959

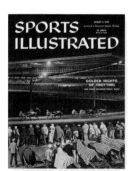

HARNESS RACING
August 3, 1959

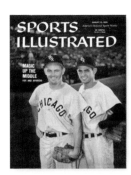

FOX & APARICIO
August 10, 1959

ANN QUAST
August 17, 1959

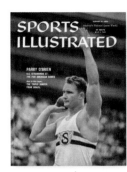

STAVROS NIARCHOS
August 24, 1959

PARRY O'BRIEN
August 31, 1959

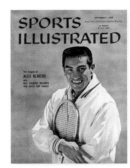

ALEX OLMEDO
September 7, 1959

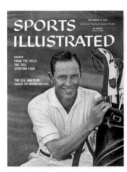

CHARLIE COE
September 14, 1959

COLLEGE FOOTBALL
September 21, 1959

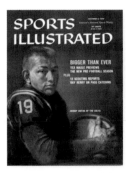

CHICAGO WHITE SOX
September 28, 1959

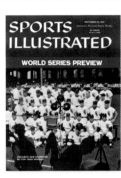

JOHNNY UNITAS
October 5, 1959

DUCK HUNTING
October 12, 1959

RACING AT LIME ROCK
October 19, 1959

GEORGE IZO
October 26, 1959

GOLF AT ELDORADO
November 2, 1959

TEXAS FOOTBALL
November 9, 1959

DAYTONA SPORTS CARS
November 16, 1959

SKIING IN ALTA
November 23, 1959

RETRIEVER CHAMPION
November 30, 1959

COLLEGE BASKETBALL
December 7, 1959

TOM WATSON FAMILY
December 14, 1959

YEAR IN REVIEW
December 21, 1959

Sports Illustrated

MAY 5, 1969   50 CENTS

ALI-CLAY

THE ONCE
– AND FUTURE ?–
KING

1960–1969

A French Twist

BY FRANK DEFORD

IT IS OFTEN SAID THAT THE '60S in the U.S. didn't really begin until after President Kennedy was assassinated late in '63. At SPORTS ILLUSTRATED, though, the '60s began right on time. Andre Laguerre was promoted to managing editor in May 1960 and immediately reconstituted the magazine, its pages and its purpose. Since the magazine had lost some $20 million in the '50s—full-blooded Yankee dollars then—and appeared dead in the water, it's even fair to say that the Frenchman saved America's sports weekly.

In reorganizing the staff and the way the magazine was laid out, Laguerre brought a whole new vision to the enterprise. It wasn't really complicated, though. He simply decided that were a popular weekly sports magazine to prosper, well, it had to be about *sports*. The fashions and the yachts and the horse shows were elbowed to the fringes, while the sweaty *déclassé* sports like boxing and basketball were pushed to the fore.

Most significantly, Laguerre not only took note of the rise of the NFL, but also saw the obvious juxtaposition: Pro football was a weekly game; SPORTS ILLUSTRATED was a weekly magazine. It was wonderfully symbiotic, and by 1963 Laguerre blessed the relationship by bypassing all the mere athletes and ordaining Pete Rozelle, the young NFL commissioner, as the magazine's Sportsman of the Year.

That decision upset some of the more traditional staff, but Laguerre was a magical leader, and while he may have been the very soul of bonhomie at the bar amidst his buddies, he displayed enough mystery and reserve to become an almost ecclesiastical figure. The man had a past: He had been plucked out of the burning waters off Dunkirk and become an aide to Charles de Gaulle. Laguerre also had a bias: He loved good writing. He always wore a white shirt, unbuttoned at the collar, black tie, sleeves rolled up, and he paced the halls wielding the taped shaft of a golf club. He was not exactly loved and not exactly feared, but he was followed.

Laguerre did not possess a good eye for design, but he was saved in that regard by his most important appointment—Dick Gangel, the art director. Pencil-thin, cocksure, a former fighter pilot, Gangel improved the appearance of the magazine as much as Laguerre did the substance. Under Gangel, the jock magazine published more fine art than any periodical in the country. New photographers, including a couple who broke in literally as teenagers—Walter Iooss Jr. and Neil Leifer—took the pictures up several notches.

This was a period that David Halberstam would call "the golden age of magazines"—an interregnum between the fading newspaper hegemony and the inevitable sovereign takeover by television—and there were many critics who would proclaim SI the most dependably well-written magazine in the land. Laguerre gave his writers a long leash, so there was a tremendous variety of style and tone. Nothing illustrated this better than the arrival of two new writers: Dan Jenkins, a Texas wisecracker who made good fun of fun and games, and Mark Kram, a Baltimorean and Mencken acolyte, whose prose invariably located sport somewhere between irony and tragedy.

Laguerre's favorite, though, was Jack Olsen, a versatile, dog-with-a-bone reporter, whose stunning five-part series in 1968, THE BLACK ATHLETE—A SHAMEFUL STORY, provoked about equal portions of acclaim and anger. Much of the latter came from the higher-ups at Time Inc., who were appalled at how unrelentingly honest Olsen—and SPORTS ILLUSTRATED—had been in dealing with a subject, race, that was whipsawing America at the time.

Oh yes, it was also in the '60s that Laguerre gave the world the Swimsuit Issue. Actually, he didn't plan that. He just sort of stumbled on it, and it took off. Since a picture of a bathing beauty is worth a thousand words, there's no need to explain all that. It was just very lucky. But then, it was a lucky decade for SPORTS ILLUSTRATED. It was a heady time.

FRANK DEFORD *joined SI as a reporter in 1962, is still an editor-at-large and is the author of 17 books.*

1960-1969

THE PLAYERS
WITH MAGIC

LUIS APARICIO
OF THE WHITE SOX

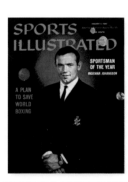

INGEMAR JOHANSSON
January 4, 1960

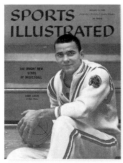

JERRY LUCAS
January 11, 1960

ART WALL
January 18, 1960

RUSSIAN SPORTS
January 25, 1960

BETSY SNITE
February 1, 1960

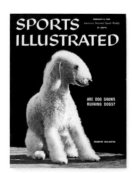

WESTMINSTER DOGS
February 8, 1960

> " OUR EDITORIAL CONCEPT *of what this magazine is trying to do is a simple one. We are trying to produce the best written and best looking weekly magazine in the world. . . . I am particularly proud of a group of young writers who are in the process of establishing names, which, believe me, will be nationally famous for years to come.* "
>
> —Andre Laguerre, *SI managing editor,* 1963

GENNADY VERONIN
February 15, 1960

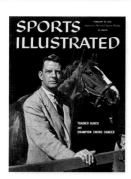

BURCH & SWORD DANCER
February 22, 1960

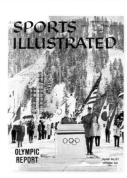

SQUAW VALLEY GAMES
February 29, 1960

SPRING TRAINING
March 7, 1960

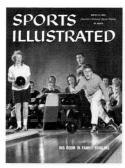

FAMILY BOWLING
March 14, 1960

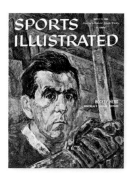

MAURICE RICHARD
March 21, 1960

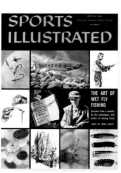

FLY-FISHING TIPS
March 28, 1960

MASTERS PREVIEW
April 4, 1960

BASEBALL PREVIEW
April 11, 1960

CARIN CONE
April 18, 1960

DALLAS LONG
April 25, 1960

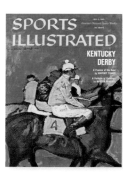

DERBY PREVIEW
May 2, 1960

BOATING IN ALASKA
May 9, 1960

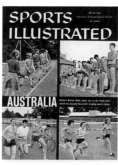

AUSTRALIAN SPORTS
May 16, 1960

CHARLES GOREN
May 23, 1960

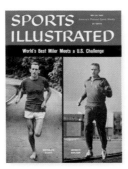

MILE SHOWDOWN
May 30, 1960

RED SCHOENDIENST
June 6, 1960

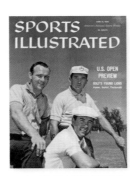

U.S. OPEN PREVIEW
June 13, 1960

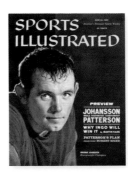

INGEMAR JOHANSSON
June 20, 1960

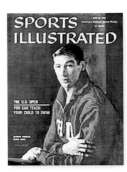

GLENN DAVIS
June 27, 1960

COMISKEY PARK
July 4, 1960

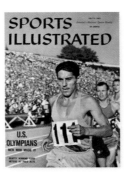

JIM BEATTY
July 11, 1960

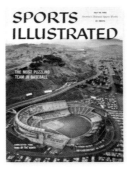

SAN FRANCISCO GIANTS
July 18, 1960

PACIFIC REGATTA
July 25, 1960

MIKE TROY
August 1, 1960

DICK GROAT
August 8, 1960

OLYMPIC PREVIEW
August 15, 1960

BARBARA McINTIRE
August 22, 1960

HIMALAYAN CLIMB
August 29, 1960

SUMMER OLYMPICS
September 5, 1960

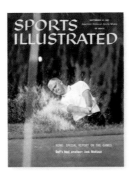

JACK NICKLAUS
September 12, 1960

COLLEGE FOOTBALL
September 19, 1960

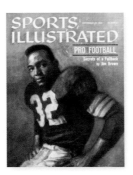

JIM BROWN
September 26, 1960

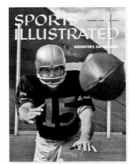

BOB SCHLOREDT
October 3, 1960

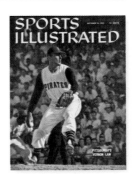

VERNON LAW
October 10, 1960

SPORTS FASHION
October 17, 1960

FOOTBALL VIOLENCE
October 24, 1960

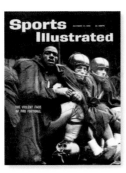

JACK BRABHAM
October 31, 1960

THE ANTI-GOURMET
November 7, 1960

BOBBY HULL
November 14, 1960

SKIING SPORTSWEAR
November 21, 1960

JOE BELLINO
November 28, 1960

SAM SNEAD
December 5, 1960

BASKETBALL PREVIEW
December 12, 1960

NORM VAN BROCKLIN
December 19, 1960

THE KENNEDYS
December 26, 1960

ARNOLD PALMER
January 9, 1961

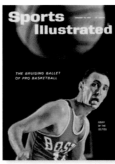

BOB COUSY
January 16, 1961

CROSBY GOLF
January 23, 1961

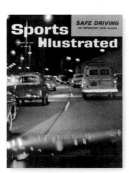

SAFE DRIVING
January 30, 1961

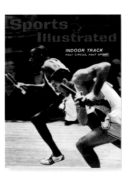

INDOOR TRACK
February 6, 1961

LAURENCE OWEN
February 13, 1961

BILLY CASPER
February 20, 1961

BOBSLEDDING
February 27, 1961

SPRING TRAINING
March 6, 1961

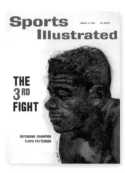

FLOYD PATTERSON
March 13, 1961

SKYDIVING
March 20, 1961

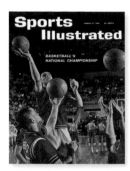

OHIO STATE
March 27, 1961

MASTERS PREVIEW
April 3, 1961

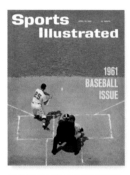

BASEBALL PREVIEW
April 10, 1961

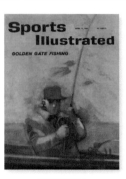

FISHING
April 17, 1961

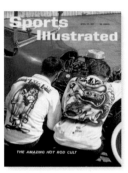

HOT ROD CULTURE
April 24, 1961

DERBY PREVIEW
May 1, 1961

GARY PLAYER
May 8, 1961

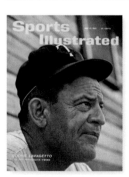

COOKIE LAVAGETTO
May 15, 1961

SNORKELING
May 22, 1961

INDY 500 PREVIEW
May 29, 1961

OCEAN RACING
June 5, 1961

U.S. OPEN PREVIEW
June 12, 1961

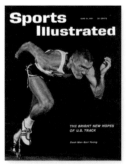

EARL YOUNG
June 19, 1961

ERNIE BROGLIO
June 26, 1961

SWIMMING
July 3, 1961

TENNIS IN CRISIS
July 10, 1961

VALERI BRUMEL
July 17, 1961

FISHING
July 24, 1961

BANG-BANG PLAYS
July 31, 1961

LISA LANE
August 7, 1961

MURRAY ROSE
August 14, 1961

JUDY TORLUEMKE
August 21, 1961

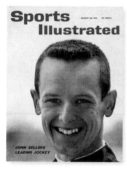

JOHN SELLERS
August 28, 1961

U.S. OPEN TENNIS
September 4, 1961

DEANE BEMAN
September 11, 1961

COLLEGE FOOTBALL
September 18, 1961

BART STARR
September 25, 1961

ROGER MARIS
October 2, 1961

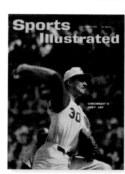

JOEY JAY
October 9, 1961

TERRY BAKER
October 16, 1961

JON ARNETT
October 23, 1961

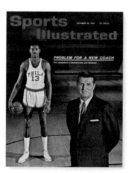

WILT CHAMBERLAIN
October 30, 1961

KELSO
November 6, 1961

TOM McNEELEY
November 13, 1961

Y.A. TITTLE
November 20, 1961

JIMMY SAXTON
November 27, 1961

SKIING IN ASPEN
December 4, 1961

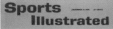
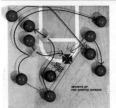

BASKETBALL STRATEGY
December 11, 1961

DAN CURRIE
December 18, 1961

FRANCINE BREAUD
December 25, 1961

JERRY LUCAS
January 8, 1962

DONALD HEAD
January 15, 1962

DOUG SANDERS
January 22, 1962

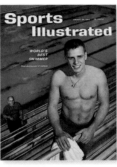

CHET JASTREMSKI
January 29, 1962

JOAN HANNAH
February 5, 1962

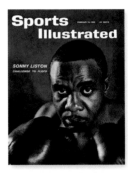

SONNY LISTON
February 12, 1962

MICKEY WRIGHT
February 19, 1962

JOHN UELSES
February 26, 1962

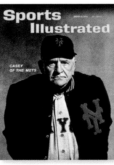

CASEY STENGEL
March 5, 1962

HORSE RACING
March 12, 1962

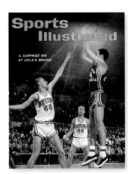

UCLA BASKETBALL
March 19, 1962

RICARDO RODRIGUEZ
March 26, 1962

ARNOLD PALMER
April 2, 1962

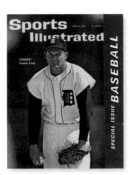

FRANK LARY
April 9, 1962

DONNA DE VARONA
April 16, 1962

JERRY SCHMIDT
April 23, 1962

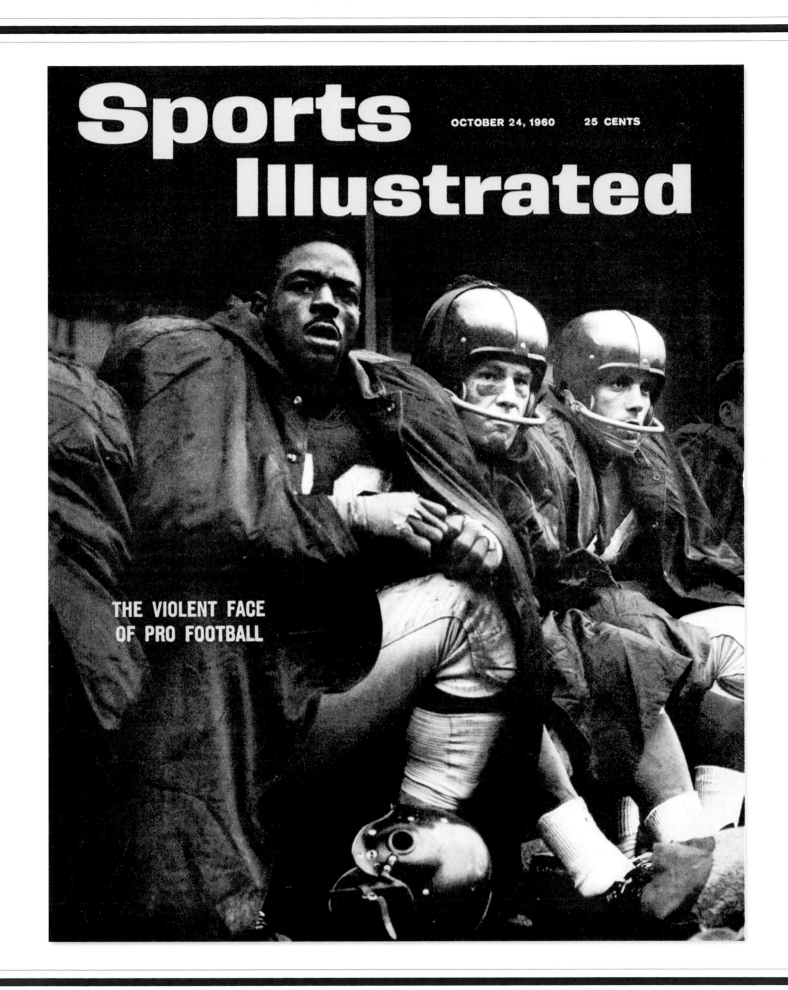

Sports Illustrated

OCTOBER 24, 1960   25 CENTS

THE VIOLENT FACE
OF PRO FOOTBALL

LUIS APARICIO
April 30, 1962

DERBY PREVIEW
May 7, 1962

GENE LITTLER
May 14, 1962

WATERSKIING
May 21, 1962

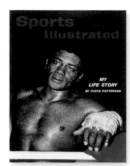

FLOYD PATTERSON
May 28, 1962

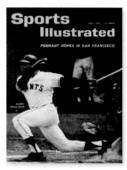

WILLIE MAYS
June 4, 1962

U.S. OPEN PREVIEW
June 11, 1962

CORNELL CREW
June 18, 1962

JACK NICKLAUS
June 25, 1962

MICKEY MANTLE
July 2, 1962

AMERICA'S CUP
July 9, 1962

IGOR TER-OVANESYAN
July 16, 1962

BARBARA McALISTER
July 23, 1962

KEN BOYER
July 30, 1962

PAUL RUNYAN
August 6, 1962

DICK FORTENBERRY
August 13, 1962

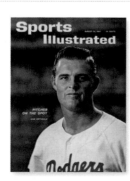

DON DRYSDALE
August 20, 1962

HELGA SCHULTZE
August 27, 1962

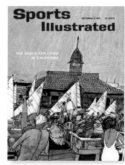

NEWPORT BEACH
September 3, 1962

TAYLOR & GREGG
September 10, 1962

SONNY LISTON
September 17, 1962

COLLEGE FOOTBALL
September 24, 1962

WORLD SERIES
October 1, 1962

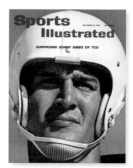

TOMMY McDONALD
October 8, 1962

SONNY GIBBS
October 15, 1962

ELK HUNTING
October 22, 1962

FRAN TARKENTON
October 29, 1962

MARY ANDERSON
November 5, 1962

SNEAD & PALMER
November 12, 1962

NICK PIETROSANTE
November 19, 1962

ARMY FOOTBALL
November 26, 1962

SKIING IN MONTANA
December 3, 1962

COTTON NASH
December 10, 1962

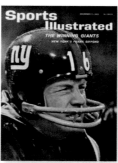

FRANK GIFFORD
December 17, 1962

ADVENTURE SPORTS
December 24, 1962

TERRY BAKER
January 7, 1963

PHIL RODGERS
January 14, 1963

PUERTO VALLARTA
January 21, 1963

HOWIE YOUNG
January 28, 1963

VALERI BRUMEL
February 4, 1963

CATHY NAGEL
February 11, 1963

JERRY BARBER
February 18, 1963

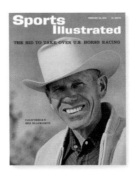

REX ELLSWORTH
February 25, 1963

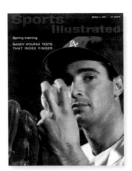

SANDY KOUFAX
March 4, 1963

CHUCK FERRIES
March 11, 1963

CINCINNATI'S TITLE
March 18, 1963

SONNY LISTON
March 25, 1963

MASTERS PREVIEW
April 1, 1963

BASEBALL PREVIEW
April 8, 1963

WOMEN'S TENNIS
April 15, 1963

MARLIN FISHING
April 22, 1963

ART MAHAFFEY
April 29, 1963

DERBY PREVIEW
May 6, 1963

YACHTING ETIQUETTE
May 13, 1963

PAUL HORNUNG
May 20, 1963

DAN GURNEY
May 27, 1963

BOB HOPE
June 3, 1963

CASSIUS CLAY
June 10, 1963

JACK NICKLAUS
June 17, 1963

ROY FACE
June 24, 1963

JULIUS BOROS
July 1, 1963

CASTING TECHNIQUES
July 8, 1963

ARNOLD PALMER
July 15, 1963

DICK GROAT
July 22, 1963

SONNY LISTON
July 29, 1963

NANCY VONDERHEIDE
August 5, 1963

ALFRED VANDERBILT
August 12, 1963

RON VANDERKELEN
August 19, 1963

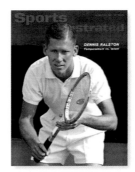

DENNIS RALSTON
August 26, 1963

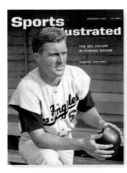

RON FAIRLY
September 2, 1963

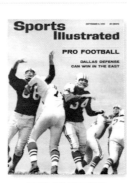

NFL PREVIEW
September 9, 1963

SAILING
September 16, 1963

GEORGE MIRA
September 23, 1963

WHITEY FORD
September 30, 1963

DEER HUNTING
October 7, 1963

RONNIE BULL
October 14, 1963

DUKE CARLISLE
October 21, 1963

HEYMAN & LUCAS
October 28, 1963

NORTHWESTERN
November 4, 1963

NFL ROUGH PLAY
November 11, 1963

SKIING AT SUGARBUSH
November 18, 1963

WILLIE GALIMORE
November 25, 1963

ROGER STAUBACH
December 2, 1963

COLLEGE BASKETBALL
December 9, 1963

LOWE & ROTE
December 16, 1963

C.K. YANG
December 23, 1963

PETE ROZELLE
January 6, 1964

WILLARD VS. DEMPSEY
January 13, 1964

BABETTE MARCH
January 20, 1964

BUDDY WERNER
January 27, 1964

BOBBY HULL
February 3, 1964

EGON ZIMMERMANN
February 10, 1964

BRIDGE
February 17, 1964

CASSIUS CLAY
February 24, 1964

STENGEL & BERRA
March 2, 1964

CLAY VS. LISTON
March 9, 1964

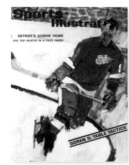

GORDIE HOWE
March 16, 1964

TONY LEMA
March 23, 1964

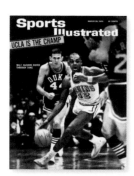

WALT HAZZARD
March 30, 1964

JACK NICKLAUS
April 6, 1964

SANDY KOUFAX
April 13, 1964

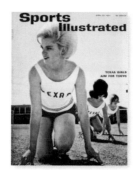

TEXAS TRACK CLUB
April 20, 1964

CLAUDE HARMON
April 27, 1964

DERBY PREVIEW
May 4, 1964

AL KALINE
May 11, 1964

JOEY GIARDELLO
May 18, 1964

FRANK HOWARD
May 25, 1964

A.J. FOYT
June 1, 1964

BILL HARTACK
June 8, 1964

U.S. OPEN PREVIEW
June 15, 1964

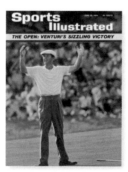

TOM O'HARA
June 22, 1964

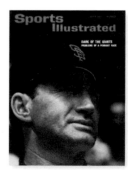

KEN VENTURI
June 29, 1964

ALVIN DARK
July 6, 1964

TENNIS INSTRUCTION
July 13, 1964

SHIRLEY MacLAINE
July 20, 1964

TOMMY McDONALD
July 27, 1964

BETSY RAWLS
August 3, 1964

JOHNNY CALLISON
August 10, 1964

DON TRULL
August 17, 1964

AMERICA'S CUP
August 24, 1964

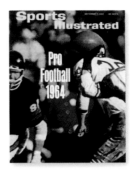

ORIOLES VS. WHITE SOX
August 31, 1964

NFL PREVIEW
September 7, 1964

JIM RYUN
September 14, 1964

JIMMY SIDLE
September 21, 1964

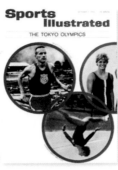

TOMMY MASON
September 28, 1964

OLYMPIC PREVIEW
October 5, 1964

DICK BUTKUS
October 12, 1964

TOKYO OLYMPICS
October 19, 1964

TOMMY HEINSOHN
October 26, 1964

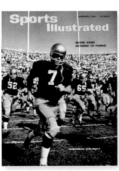

JOHN HUARTE
November 2, 1964

JOHN DAVID CROW
November 9, 1964

CLAY VS. LISTON
November 16, 1964

HELMUT FLACH
November 23, 1964

ALEX KARRAS
November 30, 1964

BILL BRADLEY
December 7, 1964

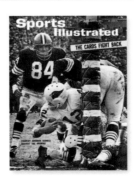

CARDINALS VS. BROWNS
December 14, 1964

KEN VENTURI
December 21, 1964

FRANK RYAN
January 4, 1965

ERNIE KOY
January 11, 1965

SUE PETERSON
January 18, 1965

BOBBY HULL
January 25, 1965

GEORGE CHUVALO
February 1, 1965

JERRY WEST
February 8, 1965

BEST U.S. GOLF HOLES
February 15, 1965

BEST U.S. GOLF HOLES II
February 22, 1965

BUNNING & BELINSKY
March 1, 1965

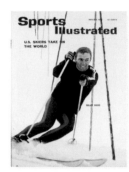

BILLY KIDD
March 8, 1965

TONY LEMA
March 15, 1965

WILLIE PASTRANO
March 22, 1965

GAIL GOODRICH
March 29, 1965

PALMER & NICKLAUS
April 5, 1965

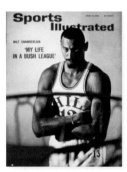

WILT CHAMBERLAIN
April 12, 1965

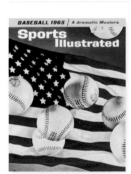

BASEBALL PREVIEW
April 19, 1965

SONNY LISTON
April 26, 1965

DERBY PREVIEW
May 3, 1965

MULDER & SMITH
May 10, 1965

BILL VEECK
May 17, 1965

TARKENTON Part 2

Sports Illustrated

JULY 24, 1967   40 CENTS

THE
SUMMER SURFERS
INVADE
HAWAII

CLAY VS. LISTON
May 24, 1965

INDY 500 PREVIEW
May 31, 1965

CLAY VS. LISTON
June 7, 1965

U.S. OPEN PREVIEW
June 14, 1965

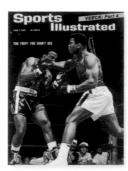

MICKEY MANTLE
June 21, 1965

HARVARD CREW
June 28, 1965

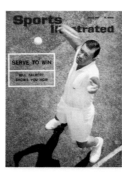

BILL TALBERT
July 5, 1965

MAURY WILLS
July 12, 1965

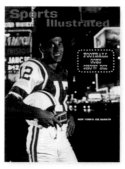

JOE NAMATH
July 19, 1965

ARNOLD PALMER
July 26, 1965

POWERBOATING
August 2, 1965

JUAN MARICHAL
August 9, 1965

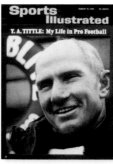

Y.A. TITTLE
August 16, 1965

TONY OLIVA
August 23, 1965

MICHEL JAZY
August 30, 1965

SUGAR RAY ROBINSON
September 6, 1965

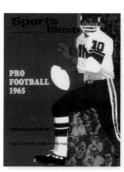

FRAN TARKENTON
September 13, 1965

FRANK SOLICH
September 20, 1965

FRANK RYAN
September 27, 1965

WORLD SERIES
October 4, 1965

KEN WILLARD
October 11, 1965

TOMMY NOBIS
October 18, 1965

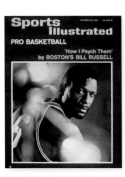

BILL RUSSELL
October 25, 1965

ST. LOUIS CARDINALS
November 1, 1965

HARRY JONES
November 8, 1965

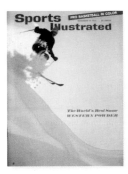

WESTERN SKIING
November 15, 1965

CLAY VS. PATTERSON
November 22, 1965

DENNIS GAUBATZ
November 29, 1965

UCLA'S ZONE PRESS
December 6, 1965

LANCE ALWORTH
December 13, 1965

SANDY KOUFAX
December 20, 1965

BOWL PREVIEWS
January 3, 1966

JIM TAYLOR
January 10, 1966

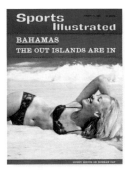

SUNNY BIPPUS
January 17, 1966

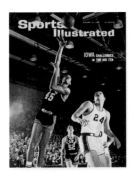

IOWA BASKETBALL
January 24, 1966

STAN MIKITA
January 31, 1966

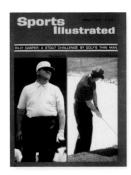

BILLY CASPER
February 7, 1966

RICK MOUNT
February 14, 1966

JEAN-CLAUDE KILLY
February 21, 1966

DUROCHER & STANKY
February 28, 1966

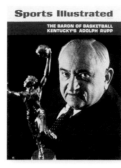

ADOLPH RUPP
March 7, 1966

RICHMOND FLOWERS
March 14, 1966

GARY PLAYER
March 21, 1966

TEXAS WESTERN WINS
March 28, 1966

MASTERS PREVIEW
April 4, 1966

CLAY VS. CHUVALO
April 11, 1966

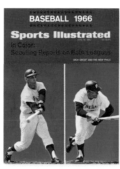

DICK GROAT
April 18, 1966

GADSBY & MIKITA
April 25, 1966

PEGGY FLEMING
May 2, 1966

JOHN HAVLICEK
May 9, 1966

KENTUCKY DERBY
May 16, 1966

SAM McDOWELL
May 23, 1966

INDIANAPOLIS 500
May 30, 1966

HOUSTON ASTROS
June 6, 1966

KEN VENTURI
June 13, 1966

JIM RYUN
June 20, 1966

BILLY CASPER
June 27, 1966

OCEAN SAILING
July 4, 1966

ANDY ETCHEBARREN
July 11, 1966

EAST COAST SURFING
July 18, 1966

REDSKINS REVIVAL
July 25, 1966

JIM RYUN
August 1, 1966

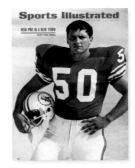

FRANK EMANUEL
August 8, 1966

BEAR BRYANT
August 15, 1966

HORNUNG & TAYLOR
August 22, 1966

ARTHUR ASHE
August 29, 1966

HARRY WALKER
September 5, 1966

BUKICH & SAYERS
September 12, 1966

GARY BEBAN
September 19, 1966

GAYLORD PERRY
September 26, 1966

LOS ANGELES RAMS
October 3, 1966

THE O'S ROBINSONS
October 10, 1966

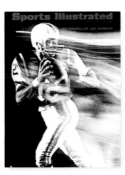

JOE NAMATH
October 17, 1966

ELGIN BAYLOR
October 24, 1966

BART STARR
October 31, 1966

TERRY HANRATTY
November 7, 1966

TOP U.S. SKI SLOPES
November 14, 1966

ROSS FICHTNER
November 21, 1966

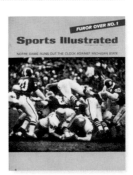

NOTRE DAME VS. MSU
November 28, 1966

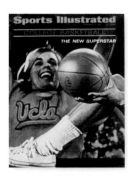

LEW ALCINDOR
December 5, 1966

BOSTON PATRIOTS
December 12, 1966

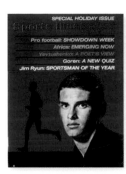

JIM RYUN
December 19, 1966

BOWL PREVIEW
January 2, 1967

BART STARR
January 9, 1967

MARILYN TINDALL
January 16, 1967

MAX McGEE
January 23, 1967

ROD GILBERT
January 30, 1967

MUHAMMAD ALI
February 6, 1967

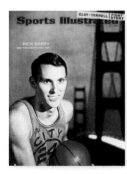

RICK BARRY
February 13, 1967

BOB SEAGREN
February 20, 1967

WALTERS & THOMFORDE
February 27, 1967

ARNOLD PALMER
March 6, 1967

JIM NASH
March 13, 1967

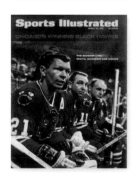

STAN MIKITA
March 20, 1967

JEAN-CLAUDE KILLY
March 27, 1967

LEW ALCINDOR
April 3, 1967

JACK NICKLAUS
April 10, 1967

MAURY WILLS
April 17, 1967

RICK BARRY
April 24, 1967

JIM HALL
May 1, 1967

BERRY & MANTLE
May 8, 1967

L.A. DODGERS
May 15, 1967

TOMMIE SMITH
May 22, 1967

INDY 500 PREVIEW
May 29, 1967

AL KALINE
June 5, 1967

BILLY CASPER
June 12, 1967

JOE HARRIS
June 19, 1967

JACK NICKLAUS
June 26, 1967

ROBERTO CLEMENTE
July 3, 1967

MUHAMMAD ALI
July 10, 1967

FRAN TARKENTON
July 17, 1967

SURFING IN HAWAII
July 24, 1967

THE SPITBALL
July 31, 1967

GAY BREWER
August 7, 1967

CUOZZO & TAYLOR
August 14, 1967

CARL YASTRZEMSKI
August 21, 1967

AMERICA'S CUP
August 28, 1967

TIM McCARVER
September 4, 1967

COLLEGE FOOTBALL
September 11, 1967

TOMMY MASON
September 18, 1967

NINO BENVENUTI
September 25, 1967

TEXAS VS. USC
October 2, 1967

MIKE PHIPPS
October 9, 1967

LOU BROCK
October 16, 1967

NBA PREVIEW
October 23, 1967

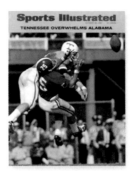

ALABAMA VS. TENNESSEE
October 30, 1967

DAN REEVES
November 6, 1967

OLYMPIC PREVIEW
November 13, 1967

BEBAN & SIMPSON
November 20, 1967

JIM HART
November 27, 1967

COLLEGE BASKETBALL
December 4, 1967

BOBBY ORR
December 11, 1967

ROMAN GABRIEL
December 18, 1967

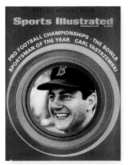

CARL YASTRZEMSKI
December 25, 1967

NFL PLAYOFFS
January 8, 1968

TURIA MAU
January 15, 1968

VINCE LOMBARDI
January 22, 1968

HAYES VS. ALCINDOR
January 29, 1968

OLYMPIC PREVIEW
February 5, 1968

BOBBY HULL
February 12, 1968

PEGGY FLEMING
February 19, 1968

CURTIS TURNER
February 26, 1968

PETE MARAVICH
March 4, 1968

BASEBALL'S ROOKIES
March 11, 1968

BILL BRADLEY
March 18, 1968

JULIUS BOROS
March 25, 1968

LEW ALCINDOR
April 1, 1968

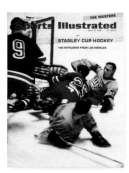

LOS ANGELES KINGS
April 8, 1968

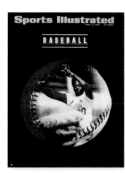

LOU BROCK
April 15, 1968

DE VICENZO & GOALBY
April 22, 1968

BAYLOR & WEST
April 29, 1968

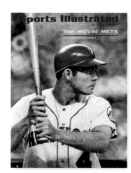

RON SWOBODA
May 6, 1968

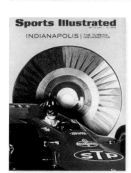

INDY 500 PREVIEW
May 13, 1968

DERBY DRUG SCANDAL
May 20, 1968

PETE ROSE
May 27, 1968

DAVE PATRICK
June 3, 1968

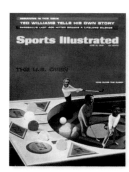

U.S. OPEN PREVIEW
June 10, 1968

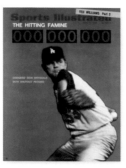
DON DRYSDALE
June 17, 1968

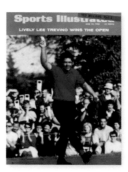
LEE TREVINO
June 24, 1968

THE BLACK ATHLETE
July 1, 1968

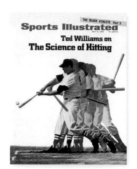
TED WILLIAMS
July 8, 1968

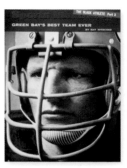
RAY NITSCHKE
July 15, 1968

MARK SPITZ
July 22, 1968

DENNY McLAIN
July 29, 1968

STANLEY DANCER
August 5, 1968

PAUL BROWN
August 12, 1968

CURT FLOOD
August 19, 1968

ROD LAVER
August 26, 1968

KEN HARRELSON
September 2, 1968

LEROY KEYES
September 9, 1968

DON MEREDITH
September 16, 1968

DENNY McLAIN
September 23, 1968

RYUN & KEINO
September 30, 1968

ST. LOUIS CARDINALS
October 7, 1968

O.J. SIMPSON
October 14, 1968

OLYMPIC PREVIEW
October 21, 1968

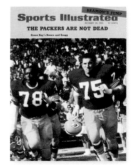
GREEN BAY PACKERS
October 28, 1968

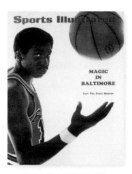

EARL MONROE
November 4, 1968

BRUCE JANKOWSKI
November 11, 1968

JEAN-CLAUDE KILLY
November 18, 1968

EARL MORRALL
November 25, 1968

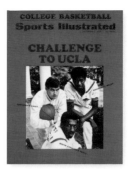

COLLEGE BASKETBALL
December 2, 1968

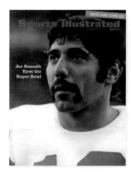

JOE NAMATH
December 9, 1968

COLTS VS. PACKERS
December 16, 1968

BILL RUSSELL
December 23, 1968

TOM MATTE
January 6, 1969

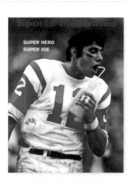

JAMEE BECKER
January 13, 1969

JOE NAMATH
January 20, 1969

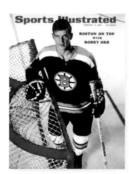

WILT CHAMBERLAIN
January 27, 1969

BOBBY ORR
February 3, 1969

BUD OGDEN
February 10, 1969

BOB LUNN
February 17, 1969

NBA'S TIGHT RACE
February 24, 1969

VINCE LOMBARDI
March 3, 1969

TRACK SCANDAL
March 10, 1969

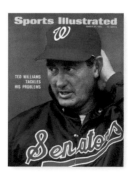

TED WILLIAMS
March 17, 1969

GUERIN & MULLINS
March 24, 1969

LEW ALCINDOR
March 31, 1969

RED BERENSON
April 7, 1969

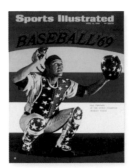

BILL FREEHAN
April 14, 1969

GEORGE ARCHER
April 21, 1969

BILL RUSSELL
April 28, 1969

MUHAMMAD ALI
May 5, 1969

JOHN HAVLICEK
May 12, 1969

L.A. DODGERS
May 19, 1969

GRIZZLY BEARS
May 26, 1969

WATER SPORTS
June 2, 1969

LEE TREVINO
June 9, 1969

JOE NAMATH
June 16, 1969

ATHLETES & DRUGS
June 23, 1969

RON SANTO
June 30, 1969

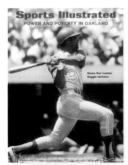

REGGIE JACKSON
July 7, 1969

O.J. SIMPSON
July 14, 1969

BILLY MARTIN
July 21, 1969

JURGENSEN & LOMBARDI
July 28, 1969

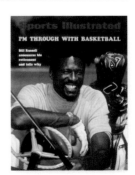

BILL RUSSELL
August 4, 1969

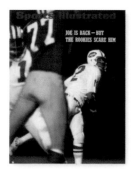

JOE NAMATH
August 11, 1969

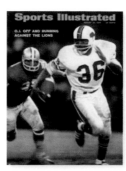

HANK AARON
August 18, 1969

O.J. SIMPSON
August 25, 1969

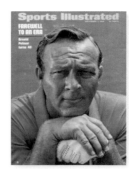

ARNOLD PALMER
September 1, 1969

ROSE & BANKS
September 8, 1969

OHIO STATE FOOTBALL
September 15, 1969

JIM TURNER
September 22, 1969

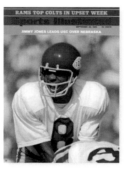

JIMMY JONES
September 29, 1969

FRANK ROBINSON
October 6, 1969

BRUCE KEMP
October 13, 1969

BROOKS ROBINSON
October 20, 1969

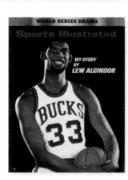

LEW ALCINDOR
October 27, 1969

MINNESOTA VIKINGS
November 3, 1969

STEVE OWENS
November 10, 1969

SKIING IN ITALY
November 17, 1969

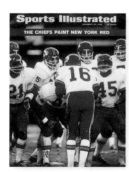

KANSAS CITY CHIEFS
November 24, 1969

PETE MARAVICH
December 1, 1969

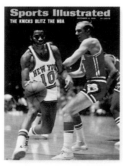

WALT FRAZIER
December 8, 1969

JAMES STREET
December 15, 1969

TOM SEAVER
December 22, 1969

Sports Illustrated

JUNE 17, 1974   60 CENTS

SUPERDUPERSTAR

Reggie Jackson

1970–1979

It All Went 'Boom'

BY PETER CARRY

IN THE JULY 17, 1978 ISSUE, SPORTS ILLUSTRATED ran the longest story in its history, a 25,000-word bruiser that took up almost 32 pages, more than half the editorial space in the magazine. The subject was a new phenomenon that senior writer Ray Kennedy christened *Moneyball*. In that piece and two slightly shorter ones in the next two issues, Kennedy was off in his analysis—that big bucks might ruin our national pastimes—but dead right on the substance: That spectator sports were becoming a huge business that would sit squarely atop the hierarchy of American cultural life. The opera? The ballet? The symphony? *Fahgettaboutem*. By the end of the decade, only a few rockers and movie stars could compete with athletes when it came to exciting public passion and cashing in on it. And no diversion could match sports when it came to engaging the hearts, minds and pocketbooks of its fans. Sports boomed in the U.S. in the 1970s, and SI exploded right along with it.

The fuse was lit on Jan. 16, 1970 when St. Louis Cardinals outfielder Curt Flood filed suit to challenge baseball's reserve clause. Flood lost his battle to become a free agent, but he set in motion a series of events that resulted in players in almost all pro sports quickly gaining the right he had been denied.

Free agency turned out to be anything but free for franchise owners. Before 1970, $100,000 was something of an unofficial max salary in team sports. By '77, the two best-paid team-sport stars, the NFL's O.J. Simpson and the NBA's Kareem Abdul-Jabbar, earned $733,358 and $625,000, respectively.

Doomsayers feared that skyrocketing ticket prices—driven by those rising salaries—and the players' willingness to switch teams at the drop of a million bucks would alienate fans and send sports into a death spiral. Even one of the greatest scorers in *Moneyball*, NBA star Elvin Hayes, felt compelled to say, "No athlete is worth the money he's getting, even me."

But something counterintuitive was taking place, and the marketing gurus—the people who fuel demand for any product—figured it out. Big contracts made athletes more glamorous than ever. Soon O.J. was running through airports for Hertz and Joe Namath was getting creamed by Farrah Fawcett for Noxema. In turn the new independence that came with those endorsement deals only made the players seem more Olympian. When such heroes met on the field, theirs became a more titanic contest. Jack up the ratings. Crank up the ad revenues. Let's play Moneyball!

In a poll SI commissioned to accompany Kennedy's series, 87% of those questioned agreed that there was too much emphasis on money in sports. But 73% also said that they forgot about filthy lucre once the games began. So salaries and TV rights fees just kept growing. Stars became superstars, and one leading measure of star power was the cover of SPORTS ILLUSTRATED. When SI's Roy Blount Jr. profiled Reggie Jackson in the June 17, 1974 issue he coined a whole new category for the A's outfielder: SUPERDUPERSTAR.

Kennedy's *Moneyball* series was the brainchild of Roy Terrell, SI's managing editor for most of the 1970s. A former Marine pilot from Kingsville, Texas, Terrell had come to SI from the *Corpus Christi Caller-Times* and had worked under Andre Laguerre as an editor for a dozen years. His decision to examine in depth the role of money in sports was a daring one at a time when most editors deemed the subject too dense and irksome to be of interest to fans. What he got for his effort was the most distinguished work of his tenure.

And in a way, Terrell played Moneyball too. In 1970 SI had been in existence for 16 years and had only been profitable for six of them. In the last year of the decade, when Terrell, a world-record-holding fisherman, retired to concentrate on catching bonefish in the waters off Florida, SI's ad revenue alone was $122 million. That made it the fourth-largest moneymaker among all U.S. magazines. SI had become a publishing behemoth, and an institution.

PETER CARRY *joined the staff of SI as a summer intern in 1963 and retired as executive editor in 2003.*

1970–1979

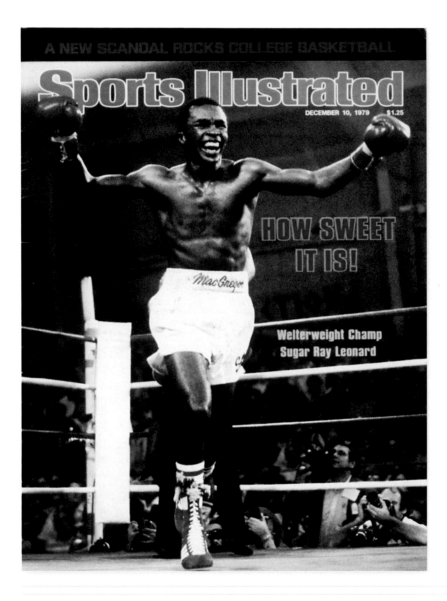

A NEW SCANDAL ROCKS COLLEGE BASKETBALL

Sports Illustrated

DECEMBER 10, 1979 $1.25

HOW SWEET IT IS!

Welterweight Champ
Sugar Ray Leonard

70 ›🕨

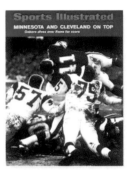

DAVE OSBORN
January 5, 1970

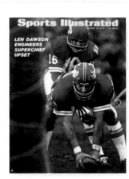

CHERYL TIEGS
January 12, 1970

LEN DAWSON
January 19, 1970

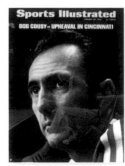

BOB COUSY
January 26, 1970

POLLUTION
February 2, 1970

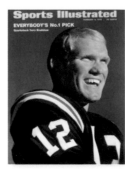

TERRY BRADSHAW
February 9, 1970

TOM McMILLEN
February 16, 1970

DENNY McLAIN
February 23, 1970

ED GIACOMIN
March 2, 1970

LEW ALCINDOR
March 9, 1970

FINAL FOUR PREVIEW
March 16, 1970

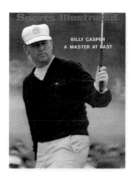

RICHIE ALLEN
March 23, 1970

GILMORE & WICKS
March 30, 1970

> **" SI HAS BECOME**
> *the Bible of the industry,*
> *and it has done so because*
> *it appreciated from*
> *the start the facts that*
> *faced printed journalism*
> *in the age of television:*
> *Don't give the scores,*
> *give the inside stories*
> *behind the scores."*
>
> —James Michener
> *Sports in America,* 1976

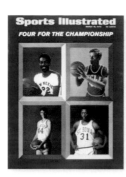

KEITH MAGNUSON
April 6, 1970

JERRY KOOSMAN
April 13, 1970

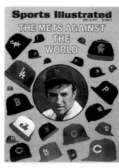

BILLY CASPER
April 20, 1970

ALCINDOR & REED
April 27, 1970

BOBBY ORR
May 4, 1970

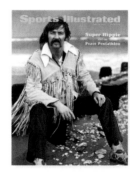

DAVID SMITH
May 11, 1970

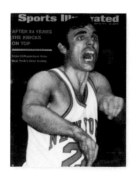

DAVE DeBUSSCHERE
May 18, 1970

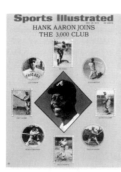

HANK AARON
May 25, 1970

NICKLAUS & PALMER
June 1, 1970

AL UNSER
June 8, 1970

STEVE PREFONTAINE
June 15, 1970

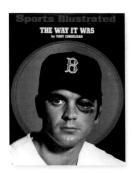

TONY CONIGLIARO
June 22, 1970

TONY JACKLIN
June 29, 1970

GEORGE FRENN
July 6, 1970

JOHNNY BENCH
July 13, 1970

JOE KAPP
July 20, 1970

WILLIE MAYS
July 27, 1970

SHORTER & MIKITENKO
August 3, 1970

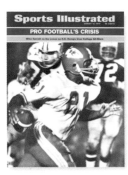

MIKE GARRETT
August 10, 1970

JOE NAMATH
August 17, 1970

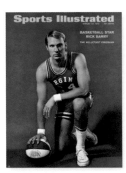

RICK BARRY
August 24, 1970

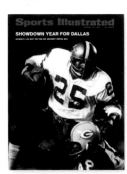

LES SHY
August 31, 1970

BUD HARRELSON
September 7, 1970

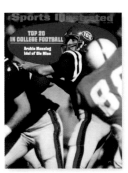

ARCHIE MANNING
September 14, 1970

DICK BUTKUS
September 21, 1970

NL PENNANT RACE
September 28, 1970

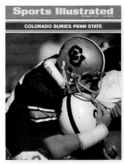

COLORADO FOOTBALL
October 5, 1970

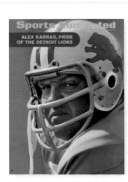

ALEX KARRAS
October 12, 1970

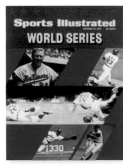

ORIOLES VS. REDS
October 19, 1970

NBA PREVIEW
October 26, 1970

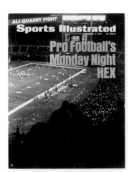

MONDAY NIGHT HEX
November 2, 1970

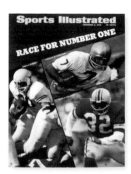

RACE FOR NO. 1
November 9, 1970

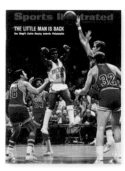

CALVIN MURPHY
November 16, 1970

GEORGE BLANDA
November 23, 1970

SIDNEY WICKS
November 30, 1970

ROMAN GABRIEL
December 7, 1970

STEVE WORSTER
December 14, 1970

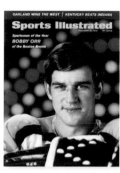

BOBBY ORR
December 21, 1970

71 >>

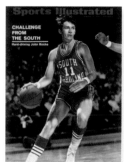

JOHN ROCHE
January 4, 1971

JOE THEISMANN
January 11, 1971

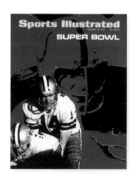

CRAIG MORTON
January 18, 1971

JIM O'BRIEN
January 25, 1971

TANNIA RUBIANO
February 1, 1971

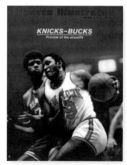

ALCINDOR & REED
February 8, 1971

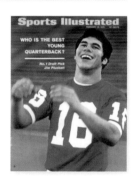

JIM PLUNKETT
February 15, 1971

DELANO MERIWETHER
February 22, 1971

ALI-FRAZIER PREVIEW
March 1, 1971

JACK NICKLAUS
March 8, 1971

ALI VS. FRAZIER
March 15, 1971

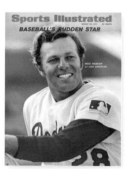

WES PARKER
March 22, 1971

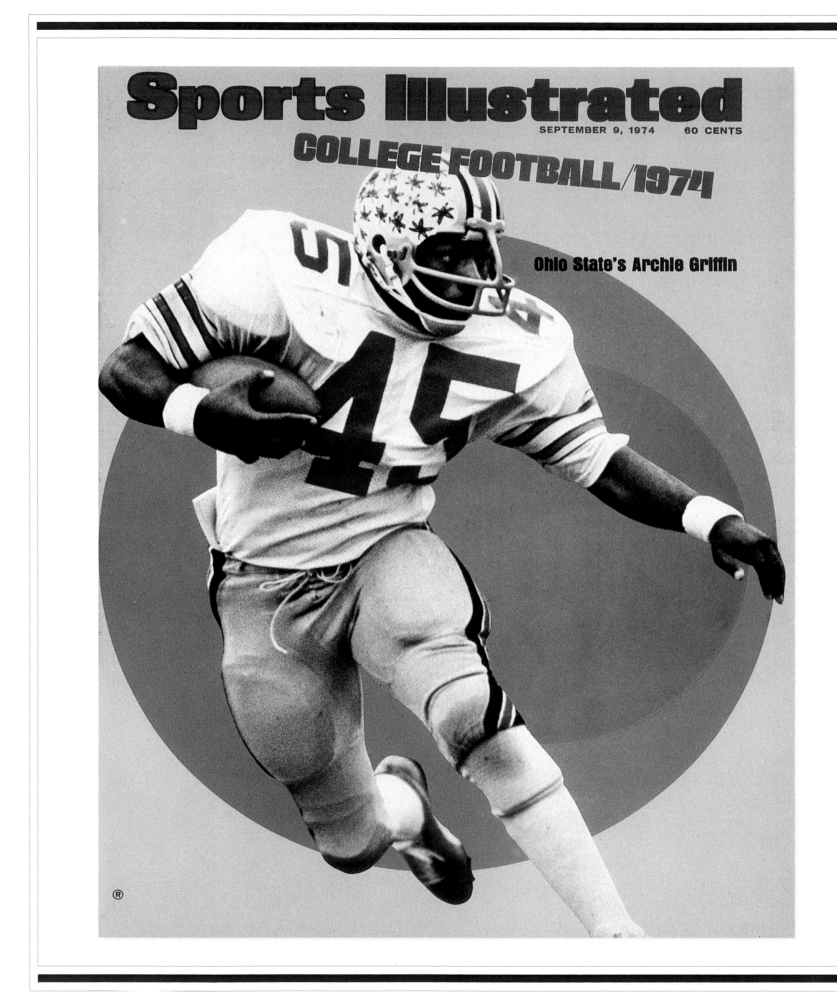

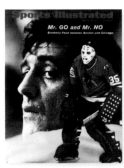

PHIL & TONY ESPOSITO
March 29, 1971

STEVE PATTERSON
April 5, 1971

BOOG POWELL
April 12, 1971

NBA PLAYOFFS
April 19, 1971

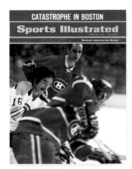

NHL PLAYOFFS
April 26, 1971

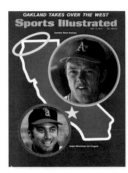

DUNCAN & FREGOSI
May 3, 1971

OSCAR ROBERTSON
May 10, 1971

JAMES McALISTER
May 17, 1971

RYUN & LIQUORI
May 24, 1971

VIDA BLUE
May 31, 1971

INDY 500
June 7, 1971

CANONERO
June 14, 1971

JERRY GROTE
June 21, 1971

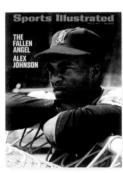

LEE TREVINO
June 28, 1971

ALEX JOHNSON
July 5, 1971

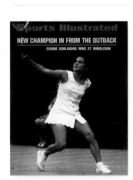

EVONNE GOOLAGONG
July 12, 1971

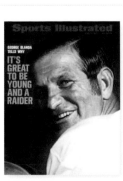

GEORGE BLANDA
July 19, 1971

MUHAMMAD ALI
July 26, 1971

WILLIE STARGELL
August 2, 1971

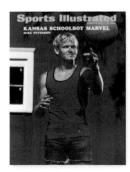

MIKE PETERSON
August 9, 1971

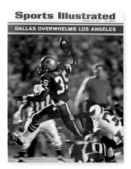

CALVIN HILL
August 16,1971

STEVE McQUEEN
August 23, 1971

FERGUSON JENKINS
August 30, 1971

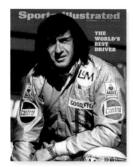

JACKIE STEWART
September 6, 1971

TOMMY CASANOVA
September 13, 1971

JOHN BRODIE
September 20, 1971

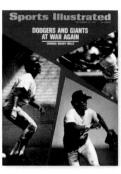

MAURY WILLS
September 27, 1971

SONNY SIXKILLER
October 4, 1971

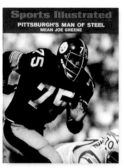

MEAN JOE GREENE
October 11, 1971

FRANK ROBINSON
October 18, 1971

BASKETBALL PREVIEW
October 25, 1971

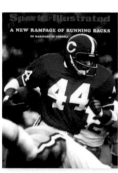

ED MARINARO
November 1, 1971

NORM BULAICH
November 8, 1971

OLYMPIC PREVIEW
November 15, 1971

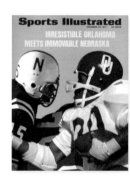

NEBRASKA–OKLAHOMA
November 22, 1971

TOM BURLESON
November 29, 1971

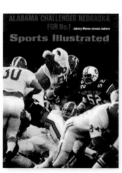

JOHNNY MUSSO
December 6, 1971

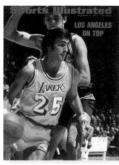

GAIL GOODRICH
December 13, 1971

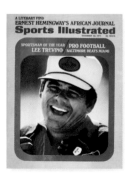

LEE TREVINO
December 20, 1971

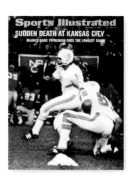

GARO YEPREMIAN
January 3, 1972

NEBRASKA FOOTBALL
January 10, 1972

SHEILA ROSCOE
January 17, 1972

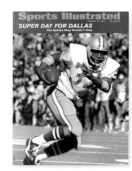

DUANE THOMAS
January 24, 1972

ANNIE HENNING
January 31, 1972

COWENS & FRAZIER
February 7, 1972

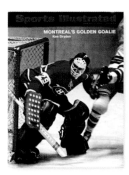

KEN DRYDEN
February 14, 1972

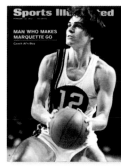

ALLIE McGUIRE
February 21, 1972

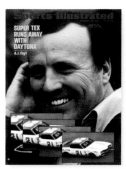

A.J. FOYT
February 28, 1972

BILL WALTON
March 6, 1972

JOHNNY BENCH
March 13, 1972

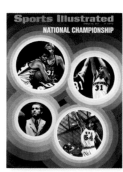

NCAA TOURNAMENT
March 20, 1972

VIDA BLUE
March 27, 1972

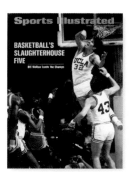

BILL WALTON
April 3, 1972

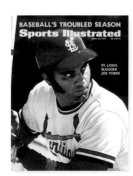

JOE TORRE
April 10, 1972

JACK NICKLAUS
April 17, 1972

NBA PLAYOFFS
April 24, 1972

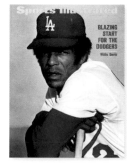

WILLIE DAVIS
May 1, 1972

ESPOSITO & ORR
May 8, 1972

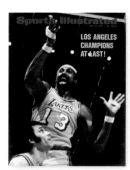

WILT CHAMBERLAIN
May 15, 1972

WILLIE MAYS
May 22, 1972

LOUIE JACOBS
May 29, 1972

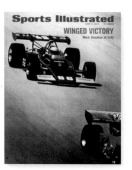

INDY 500
June 5, 1972

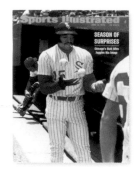

DICK ALLEN
June 12, 1972

BOBBY HULL
June 19, 1972

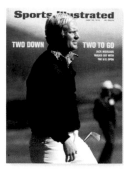

JACK NICKLAUS
June 26, 1972

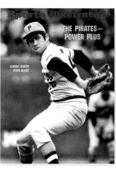

STEVE BLASS
July 3, 1972

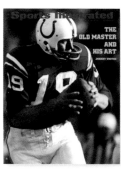

JOHNNY UNITAS
July 10, 1972

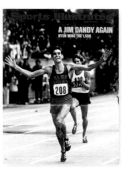

JIM RYUN
July 17, 1972

TOMMY PROTHRO
July 24, 1972

ROBYN SMITH
July 31, 1972

CSONKA & KIICK
August 7, 1972

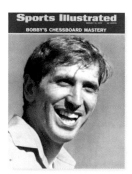

BOBBY FISCHER
August 14, 1972

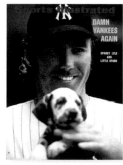

SPARKY LYLE
August 21, 1972

OLYMPIC PREVIEW
August 28, 1972

MARK SPITZ
September 4, 1972

BOB DEVANEY
September 11, 1972

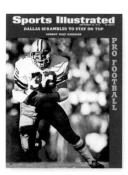

WALT GARRISON
September 18, 1972

CARLTON FISK
September 25, 1972

GREG PRUITT
October 2, 1972

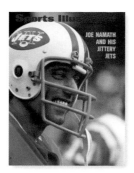

JOE NAMATH
October 9, 1972

WILT CHAMBERLAIN
October 16, 1972

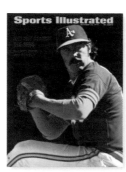

CATFISH HUNTER
October 23, 1972

DAVE & DON BUCKEY
October 30, 1972

LARRY BROWN
November 6, 1972

JOHN HAVLICEK
November 13, 1972

TERRY DAVIS
November 20, 1972

WALTER LUCKETT
November 27, 1972

STEVE SPURRIER
December 4, 1972

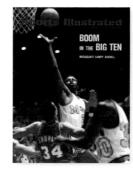

CAMPY RUSSELL
December 11, 1972

LEE ROY JORDAN
December 18, 1972

WOODEN & KING
December 25, 1972

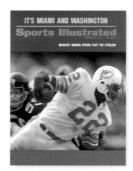

MERCURY MORRIS
January 8, 1973

DOUG COLLINS
January 15, 1973

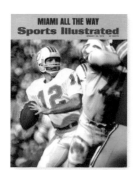

BOB GRIESE
January 22, 1973

DAYLE HADDON
January 29, 1973

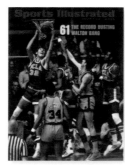

BILL WALTON
February 5, 1973

STEVE SMITH
February 12, 1973

KAREEM ABDUL-JABBAR
February 19, 1973

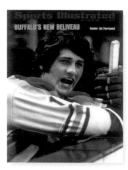

GIL PERREAULT
February 26, 1973

SPORTS ON BROADWAY
March 5, 1973

BILL MELTON
March 12, 1973

OLGA KORBUT
March 19, 1973

NCAA TOURNAMENT
March 26, 1973

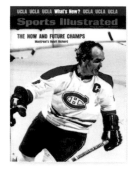

HENRI RICHARD
April 2, 1973

STEVE CARLTON
April 9, 1973

EARL MONROE
April 16, 1973

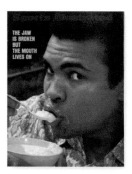

MUHAMMAD ALI
April 23, 1973

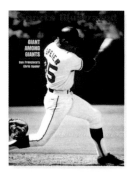

CHRIS SPEIER
April 30, 1973

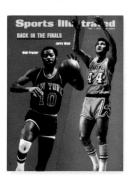

FRAZIER & WEST
May 7, 1973

MARK & SUZY SPITZ
May 14, 1973

BOBBY RIGGS
May 21, 1973

WOMEN IN SPORTS
May 28, 1973

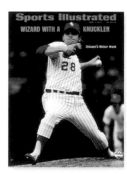

WILBUR WOOD
June 4, 1973

SECRETARIAT
June 11, 1973

GEORGE FOREMAN
June 18, 1973

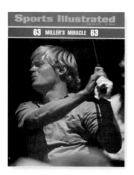

JOHNNY MILLER
June 25, 1973

MURCER & BLOMBERG
July 2, 1973

GEORGE ALLEN
July 9, 1973

BILLIE JEAN KING
July 16, 1973

TOM WEISKOPF
July 23, 1973

CARLTON FISK
July 30, 1973

JOHN MATUSZAK
August 6, 1973

YOUTH RACING
August 13, 1973

RUSSELL & OSTEEN
August 20, 1973

DUANE THOMAS
August 27, 1973

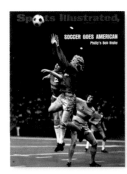

BOB RIGBY
September 3, 1973

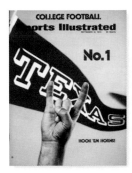

TEXAS FOOTBALL
September 10, 1973

LARRY CSONKA
September 17, 1973

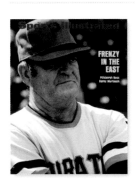

DANNY MURTAUGH
September 24, 1973

ANTHONY DAVIS
October 1, 1973

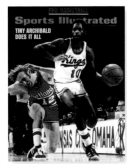

FRAN TARKENTON
October 8, 1973

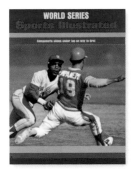

NATE ARCHIBALD
October 15, 1973

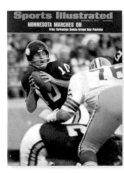

METS VS. A'S
October 22, 1973

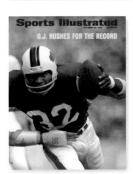

O.J. SIMPSON
October 29, 1973

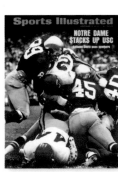

ANTHONY DAVIS
November 5, 1973

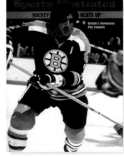

PETE MARAVICH
November 12, 1973

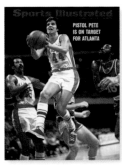

PHIL ESPOSITO
November 19, 1973

DAVID THOMPSON
November 26, 1973

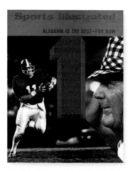

RUTLEDGE & BRYANT
December 3, 1973

ELMORE & WALTON
December 10, 1973

MARV HUBBARD
December 17, 1973

JACKIE STEWART
December 24, 1973

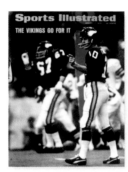

FRAN TARKENTON
January 7, 1974

JULIUS ERVING
January 14, 1974

LARRY CSONKA
January 21, 1974

ANN SIMONTON
January 28, 1974

MUHAMMAD ALI
February 4, 1974

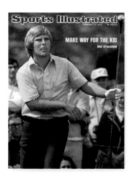

BEN CRENSHAW
February 11, 1974

JOHN HAVLICEK
February 18, 1974

BILL WALTON
February 25, 1974

JIMMY CONNORS
March 4, 1974

GORDIE HOWE
March 11, 1974

BABE RUTH
March 18, 1974

WALTON & BURLESON
March 25, 1974

THOMPSON & WALTON
April 1, 1974

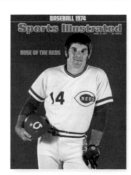

PETE ROSE
April 8, 1974

HANK AARON
April 15, 1974

GARY PLAYER
April 22, 1974

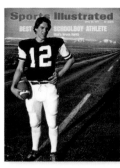

BRUCE HARDY
April 29, 1974

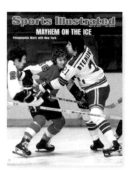

FLYERS VS. RANGERS
May 6, 1974

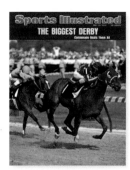

CANNONADE
May 13, 1974

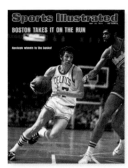

JOHN HAVLICEK
May 20, 1974

JIM WYNN
May 27, 1974

JOHNNY RUTHERFORD
June 3, 1974

JOHNNY MILLER
June 10, 1974

REGGIE JACKSON
June 17, 1974

HALE IRWIN
June 24, 1974

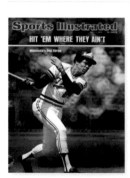

ROD CAREW
July 1, 1974

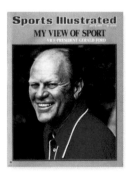

GERALD FORD
July 8, 1974

CONNORS & EVERT
July 15, 1974

LOU BROCK
July 22, 1974

TERRY BRADSHAW
July 29, 1974

NFL STRIKE
August 5, 1974

MIKE MARSHALL
August 12, 1974

LEE TREVINO
August 19, 1974

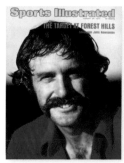

JOHN NEWCOMBE
August 26, 1974

EVEL KNIEVEL
September 2, 1974

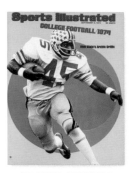

ARCHIE GRIFFIN
September 9, 1974

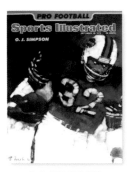

O.J. SIMPSON
September 16, 1974

JOE GILLIAM
September 23, 1974

TOM CLEMENTS
September 30, 1974

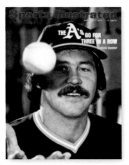

CATFISH HUNTER
October 7, 1974

ABDUL-JABBAR & WALTON
October 14, 1974

DODGERS VS. A'S
October 21, 1974

FOREMAN-ALI PREVIEW
October 28, 1974

OKLAHOMA FOOTBALL
November 4, 1974

FOREMAN VS. ALI
November 11, 1974

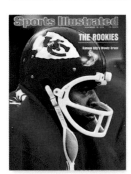

WOODY GREEN
November 18, 1974

KEN DRYDEN
November 25, 1974

COLLEGE BASKETBALL
December 2, 1974

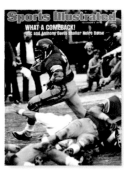

ANTHONY DAVIS
December 9, 1974

RICK BARRY
December 16, 1974

MUHAMMAD ALI
December 23, 1974

FRANCO HARRIS
January 6, 1975

BILL TILDEN
January 13, 1975

TERRY BRADSHAW
January 20, 1975

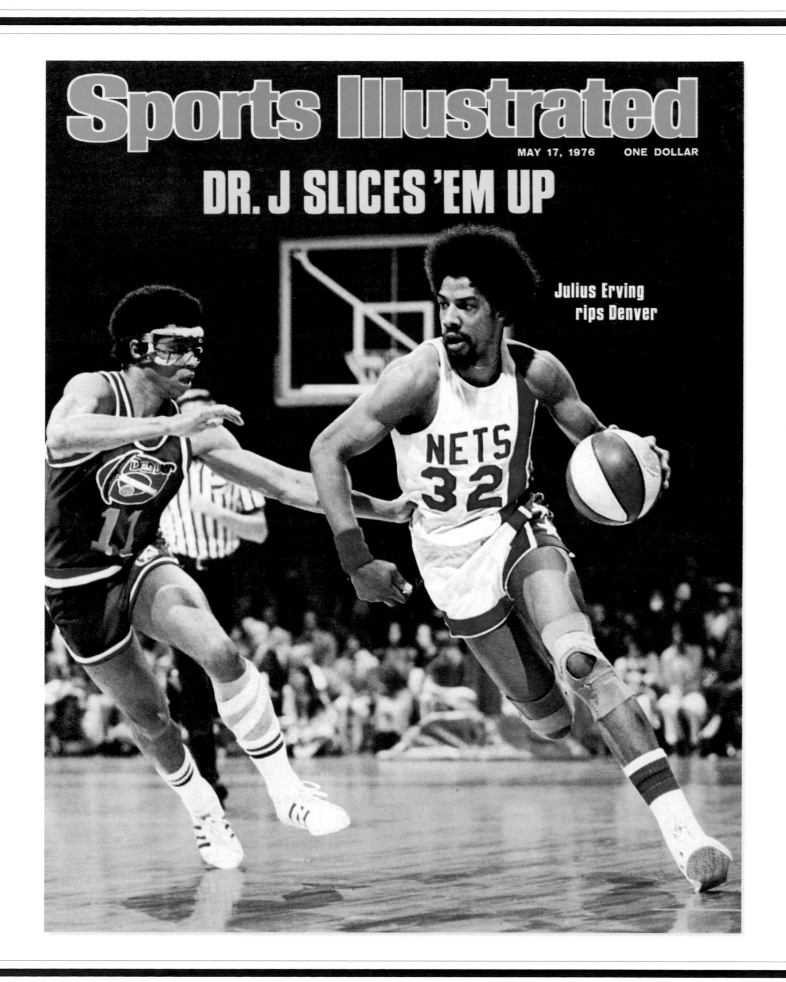

Sports Illustrated

MAY 17, 1976   ONE DOLLAR

DR. J SLICES 'EM UP

Julius Erving
rips Denver

CHERYL TIEGS
January 27, 1975

JOHN LASKOWSKI
February 3, 1975

ROGIE VACHON
February 10, 1975

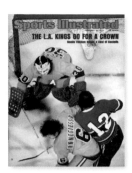
DAVE MEYERS
February 17, 1975

DOG SHOW DEBATE
February 24, 1975

REDS PITCHERS
March 3, 1975

LEE ELDER
March 10, 1975

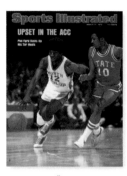
FORD & RIVERS
March 17, 1975

CHUCK WEPNER
March 24, 1975

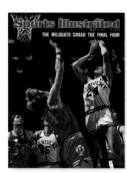
MIKE FLYNN
March 31, 1975

STEVE GARVEY
April 7, 1975

VASILI ALEXEYEV
April 14, 1975

JACK NICKLAUS
April 21, 1975

GARFIELD HEARD
April 28, 1975

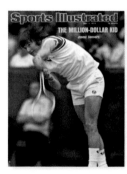
JIMMY CONNORS
May 5, 1975

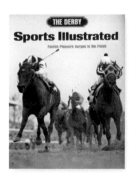
FOOLISH PLEASURE
May 12, 1975

A.J. FOYT
May 19, 1975

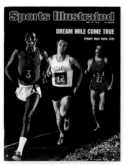
FILBERT BAYI
May 26, 1975

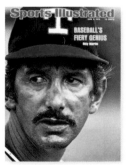
BILLY MARTIN
June 2, 1975

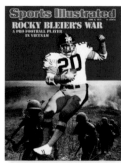
ROCKY BLEIER
June 9, 1975

NOLAN RYAN
June 16, 1975

PELÉ
June 23, 1975

LOU GRAHAM
June 30, 1975

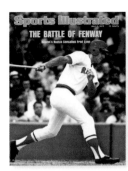

FRED LYNN
July 7, 1975

ARTHUR ASHE
July 14, 1975

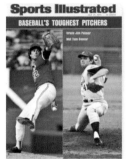

PALMER & SEAVER
July 21, 1975

WFL GRIZZLIES
July 28, 1975

TIM SHAW
August 4, 1975

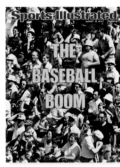

BASEBALL BOOM
August 11, 1975

JACK NICKLAUS
August 18, 1975

BART STARR
August 25, 1975

BRIAN OLDFIELD
September 1, 1975

OKLAHOMA FOOTBALL
September 8, 1975

DON KING
September 15, 1975

MEAN JOE GREENE
September 22, 1975

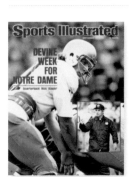

SLAGER & DEVINE
September 29, 1975

REGGIE JACKSON
October 6, 1975

ALI VS. FRAZIER III
October 13, 1975

TIANT & BENCH
October 20, 1975

GEORGE McGINNIS
October 27, 1975

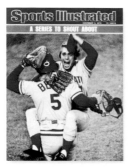

BENCH & McENANEY
November 3, 1975

FRAN TARKENTON
November 10, 1975

HOCKEY VIOLENCE
November 17, 1975

CHUCK MUNCIE
November 24, 1975

KENT BENSON
December 1, 1975

BUBBA BEAN
December 8, 1975

GEORGE FOREMAN
December 15, 1975

PETE ROSE
December 22, 1975

PRESTON PEARSON
January 5, 1976

FRANCO HARRIS
January 12, 1976

SYLVANDER TWINS
January 19, 1976

LYNN SWANN
January 26, 1976

SHEILA YOUNG
February 2, 1976

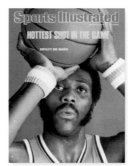

GRUNFELD & KING
February 9, 1976

FRANZ KLAMMER
February 16, 1975

BOBBY CLARKE
February 23, 1976

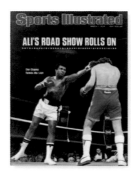

ALI VS. COOPMAN
March 1, 1976

BOB McADOO
March 8, 1976

BILL VEECK
March 15, 1976

TRACY AUSTIN
March 22, 1976

KENT BENSON
March 29, 1976

SCOTT MAY
April 5, 1976

JOE MORGAN
April 12, 1976

RAY FLOYD
April 19, 1976

EVONNE GOOLAGONG
April 26, 1976

MIKE SCHMIDT
May 3, 1976

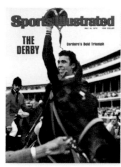

ANGEL CORDERO
May 10, 1976

JULIUS ERVING
May 17, 1976

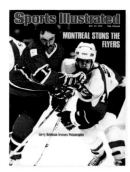

LARRY ROBINSON
May 24, 1976

PINIELLA & FISK
May 31, 1976

ADAMS & COWENS
June 7, 1976

DWIGHT STONES
June 14, 1976

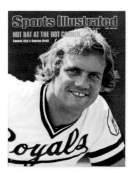

GEORGE BRETT
June 21, 1976

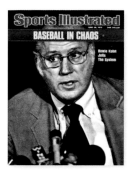

BOWIE KUHN
June 28, 1976

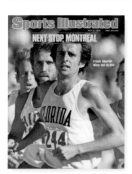

FRANK SHORTER
July 5, 1976

RANDY JONES
July 12, 1976

OLYMPIC PREVIEW
July 19, 1976

MONTREAL OLYMPICS
July 26, 1976

NADIA COMANECI
August 2, 1976

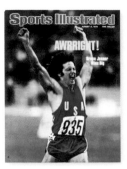

BRUCE JENNER
August 9, 1976

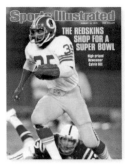

CALVIN HILL
August 16, 1976

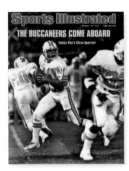

STEVE SPURRIER
August 23, 1976

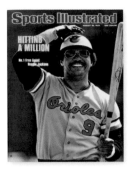

REGGIE JACKSON
August 30, 1976

RICK LEACH
September 6, 1976

BERT JONES
September 13, 1976

JIMMY CONNORS
September 20, 1976

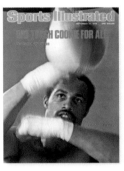

KEN NORTON
September 27, 1976

MARK MANGES
Ocotber 4, 1976

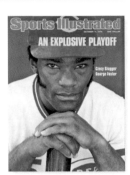

GEORGE FOSTER
October 11, 1976

CHUCK FOREMAN
October 18, 1976

COWENS & ERVING
October 25, 1976

JOHNNY BENCH
November 1, 1976

TONY DORSETT
November 8, 1976

DAVID THOMPSON
November 15, 1976

WALTER PAYTON
November 22, 1976

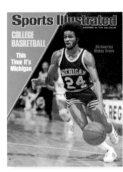

RICKEY GREEN
November 29, 1976

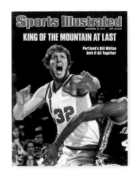

BLEIER & DAVIS
December 6, 1976

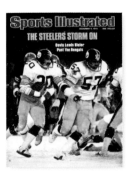

BILL WALTON
December 13, 1976

CHRIS EVERT
December 20, 1976

CLARENCE DAVIS
January 3, 1977

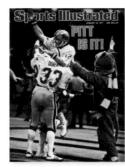

TONY DORSETT
January 10, 1977

KEN STABLER
January 17, 1977

LENA KANSBOD
January 24, 1977

BILL CARTWRIGHT
January 31, 1977

GUY LaFLEUR
February 7, 1977

KAREEM ABDUL-JABBAR
February 14, 1977

YEAR IN REVIEW
February 17, 1977

NBC'S OLYMPIC DEAL
February 21, 1977

CALE YARBOROUGH
February 28, 1977

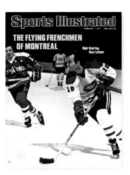

STEVE CAUTHEN
March 7, 1977

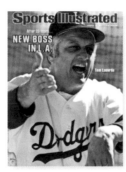

TOMMY LASORDA
March 14, 1977

GEORGE McGINNIS
March 21, 1977

BUMP WILLS
March 28, 1977

BUTCH LEE
April 4, 1977

JOE RUDI
April 11, 1977

TOM WATSON
April 18, 1977

SIDNEY WICKS
April 25, 1977

REGGIE JACKSON
May 2, 1977

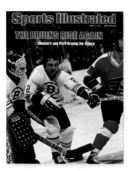

CHEEVERS & PARK
May 9, 1977

SEATTLE SLEW
May 16, 1977

WALTON & ABDUL-JABBAR
May 23, 1977

DAVE PARKER
May 30, 1977

MARK FIDRYCH
June 6, 1977

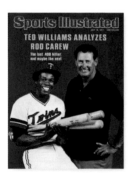

BILL WALTON
June 13, 1977

SEATTLE SLEW
June 20, 1977

TOM SEAVER
June 27, 1977

TED TURNER
July 4, 1977

BJORN BORG
July 11, 1977

CAREW & WILLIAMS
July 18, 1977

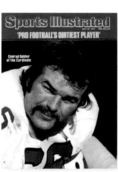

CONRAD DOBLER
July 25, 1977

COLORADO RAPIDS
August 1, 1977

CARLOS MONZON
August 8, 1977

SADAHARU OH
August 15, 1977

LANNY WADKINS
August 22, 1977

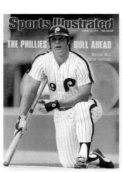

GREG LUZINSKI
August 29, 1977

ROSS BROWNER
September 5, 1977

BOIT VS. JUANTORENA
September 12, 1977

KEN STABLER
September 19, 1977

ROBERTO DURAN
September 26, 1977

BILLY SIMS
October 3, 1977

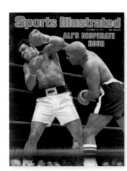

ALI VS. SHAVERS
October 10, 1977

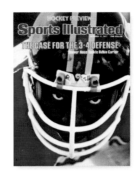

RUBIN CARTER
October 17, 1977

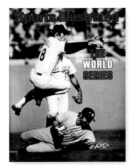

YANKEES VS. DODGERS
October 24, 1977

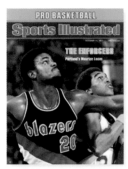

MAURICE LUCAS
October 31, 1977

"SEMI-TOUGH"
November 7, 1977

HORSE RACING FRAUD
November 14, 1977

AFC VS. NFC
November 21, 1977

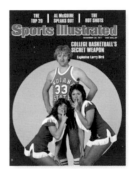

LARRY BIRD
November 28, 1977

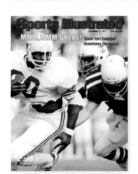

EARL CAMPBELL
December 5, 1977

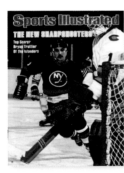

BRYAN TROTTIER
December 12, 1977

STEVE CAUTHEN
December 19, 1977

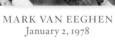

MARK VAN EEGHEN
January 2, 1978

TERRY EURICK
January 9, 1978

MARIA JOÃO
January 16, 1978

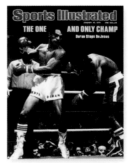

WHITE & MARTIN
January 23, 1978

DURAN VS. DeJESUS
January 30, 1978

BUERKLE & BAYI
February 6, 1978

Sports Illustrated

JUNE 20, 1977   ONE DOLLAR

RIDING HIGH AND HANDSOME

Cruguet and Slew
Win the Triple Crown

®

YEAR IN REVIEW
February 9, 1978

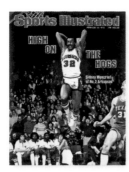

SIDNEY MONCRIEF
February 13, 1978

WALTER DAVIS
February 20, 1978

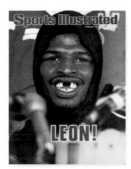

LEON SPINKS
February 27, 1978

HOUSTON McTEAR
March 6, 1978

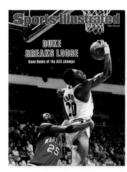

GENE BANKS
March 13, 1978

CLINT HURDLE
March 20, 1978

JACK NICKLAUS
March 27, 1978

JACK GIVENS
April 3, 1978

FOSTER & CAREW
April 10, 1978

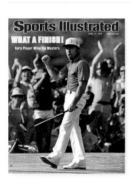

GARY PLAYER
April 17, 1978

MARK FIDRYCH
April 24, 1978

GARY PLAYER
May 1, 1978

ELVIN HAYES
May 8, 1978

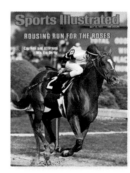

AFFIRMED
May 15, 1978

MARVIN WEBSTER
May 22, 1978

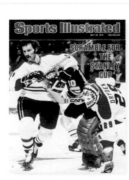

ROBINSON & DRYDEN
May 29, 1978

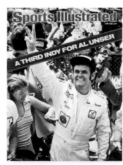

AL UNSER
June 5, 1978

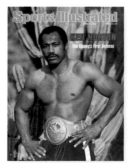

KEN NORTON
June 12, 1978

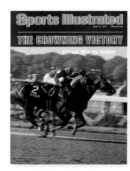

AFFIRMED
June 19, 1978

ANDY NORTH
June 26, 1978

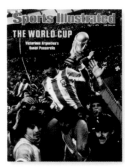

DANIEL PASSARELLA
July 3, 1978

NANCY LOPEZ
July 10, 1978

MONEY IN SPORTS
July 17, 1978

JACK NICKLAUS
July 24, 1978

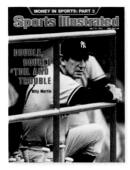

BILLY MARTIN
July 31, 1978

PETE ROSE
August 7, 1978

FOOTBALL VIOLENCE
August 14, 1978

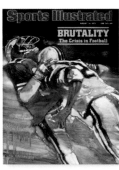

BILL WALTON
August 21, 1978

BALLOONING
August 28, 1978

ROGER STAUBACH
September 4, 1978

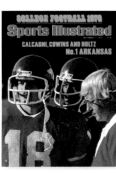

ARKANSAS FOOTBALL
September 11, 1978

JIMMY CONNORS
September 18, 1978

ALI-SPINKS II
September 25, 1978

CHARLES WHITE
October 2, 1978

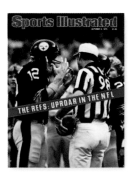

POOR OFFICIATING
October 9, 1978

MARVIN WEBSTER
October 16, 1978

YANKEES VS. DODGERS
October 23, 1978

BILL RODGERS
October 30, 1978

HORSE-RACING FIX
November 6, 1978

CHUCK FUSINA
November 13, 1978

RICK BERNS
November 20, 1978

MAGIC JOHNSON
November 27, 1978

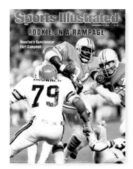

EARL CAMPBELL
December 4, 1978

JEFF LOWE
December 11, 1978

JOHN McENROE
December 18, 1978

JACK NICKLAUS
December 25, 1978

ALABAMA VS. PENN STATE
January 8, 1979

TERRY BRADSHAW
January 15, 1979

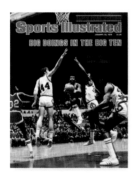

CARTER SCOTT
January 22, 1979

ROCKY BLEIER
January 29, 1979

CHRISTIE BRINKLEY
February 5, 1979

DANNY LOPEZ
February 12, 1979

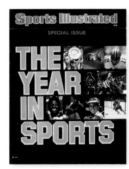

YEAR IN REVIEW
February 15, 1979

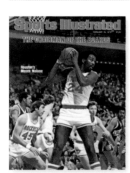

MOSES MALONE
February 19, 1979

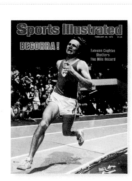

EAMONN COGHLAN
February 26, 1979

SPRING TRAINING
March 5, 1979

DUDLEY BRADLEY
March 12, 1979

HARRY CHAPPAS
March 19, 1979

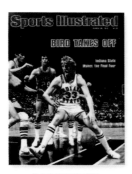

LARRY BIRD
March 26, 1979

MAGIC JOHNSON
April 2, 1979

RICE & PARKER
April 9, 1979

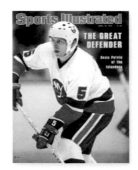

DENIS POTVIN
April 16, 1979

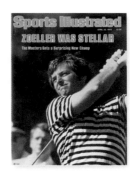

FUZZY ZOELLER
April 23, 1979

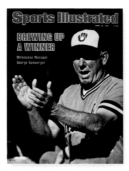

GEORGE BAMBERGER
April 30, 1979

ELVIN HAYES
May 7, 1979

RON FRANKLIN
May 14, 1979

GIORGIO CHINAGLIA
May 21, 1979

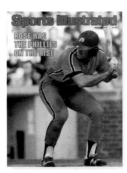

PETE ROSE
May 28, 1979

TOM WATSON
June 4, 1979

GUS WILLIAMS
June 11, 1979

EARL WEAVER
June 18, 1979

HALE IRWIN
June 25, 1979

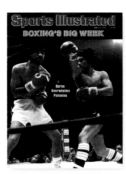

DURAN VS. PALOMINO
July 2, 1979

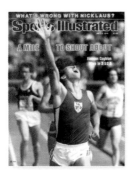

EAMONN COGHLAN
July 9, 1979

BJORN BORG
July 16, 1979

NOLAN RYAN
July 23, 1979

SEBASTIAN COE
July 30, 1979

KEN STABLER
August 6, 1979

SILVER ANNIVERSARY
August 13, 1979

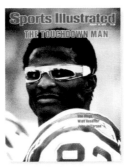

JOHN JEFFERSON
August 20, 1979

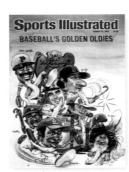

BASEBALL VETERANS
August 27, 1979

EARL CAMPBELL
September 3, 1979

WHITE & SIMS
September 10, 1979

TRACY AUSTIN
September 17, 1979

VAGAS FERGUSON
September 24, 1979

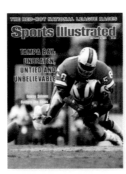

DEWEY SELMON
October 1, 1979

SHAVERS VS. HOLMES
October 8, 1979

BILL WALTON
October 15, 1979

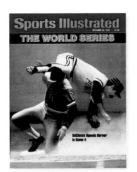

DeCINCES & GARNER
October 22, 1979

BILL RODGERS
October 29, 1979

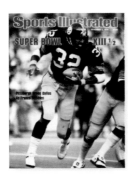

FRANCO HARRIS
November 5, 1979

COLLEGE FOOTBALL
November 12, 1979

MAGIC JOHNSON
November 19, 1979

ART SCHLICHTER
November 26, 1979

INDIANA BASKETBALL
December 3, 1979

SUGAR RAY LEONARD
December 10, 1979

RALPH SAMPSON
December 17, 1979

STARGELL & BRADSHAW
December 24, 1979

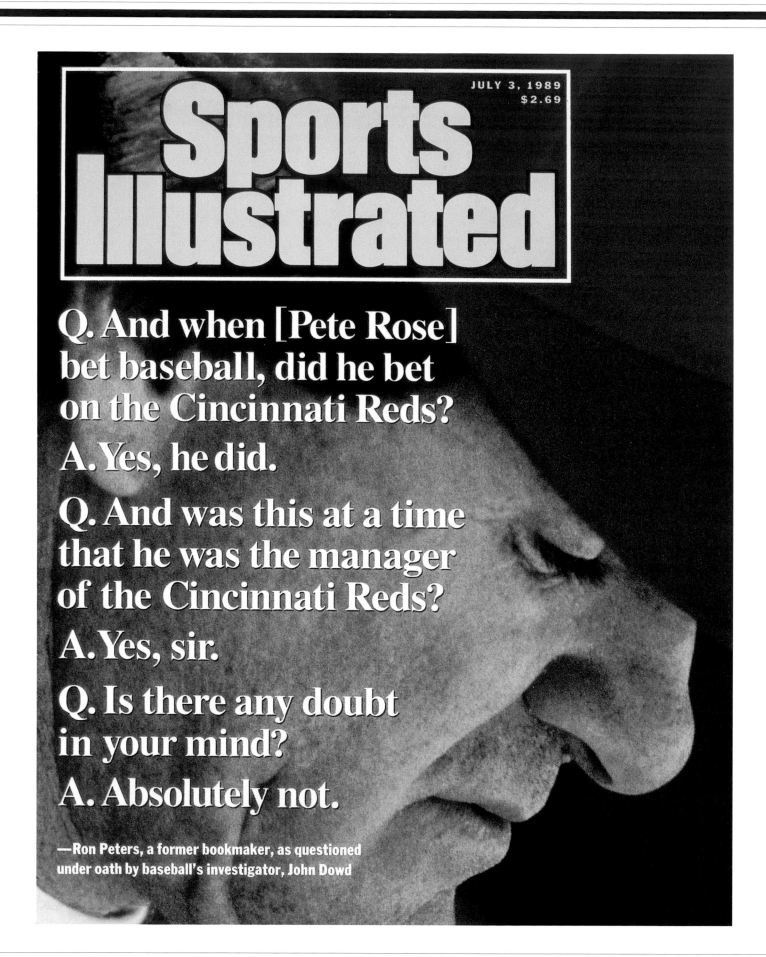

JULY 3, 1989
$2.69

Sports Illustrated

Q. And when [Pete Rose] bet baseball, did he bet on the Cincinnati Reds?

A. Yes, he did.

Q. And was this at a time that he was the manager of the Cincinnati Reds?

A. Yes, sir.

Q. Is there any doubt in your mind?

A. Absolutely not.

—Ron Peters, a former bookmaker, as questioned under oath by baseball's investigator, John Dowd

1980–1989

A Watchdog with Teeth

BY MARK MULVOY

SPORTS ILLUSTRATED HAS never been what is known in the publishing trade as a newsstand magazine; that is, a publication with a bottom line dependent on single-copy newsstand sales. By the 1980s it had grown to have a weekly base of 3.2 million subscribers and sold only another 100,000 or so copies every week on the newsstand (except, of course, in mid-February, when sales of the Swimsuit Issue soared into the millions). With such a captive and loyal audience, the managing editor had considerable license to take chances and to create covers with a timeless quality.

One SI cover in the '80s featured a close-up of a frosty mug of beer. Another had a snarling pit bull, with the stark warning: BEWARE OF THIS DOG. It turned out that the pit bull cover was one of the best-selling issues on the newsstand that year, outselling even the Super Bowl. Which, of course, got the bean counters thinking that we ought to have an annual pit bull issue to complement the Swimsuit Issue.

But the '80s will probably best be remembered at SI as the decade when the editors made it their priority to hold the people and the teams in sports accountable for their actions. Gilbert Rogin, a novelist and *New Yorker* fiction writer in an earlier life, succeeded Roy Terrell as SI's fourth managing editor, in 1979, and a series of journalistic coups followed.

In February 1981, SI's special investigators broke the news of the Boston College point-shaving scandal that rocked college basketball. In 1982, SI ran a dramatic, words-only cover heralding former Miami Dolphins lineman Don Reese's first-person account of the cocaine problem then sweeping through pro football. Pete Rozelle, the NFL commissioner at the time, later admitted that the league was unaware of the depth of its drug problems until Reese courageously revealed, among other things, that some of the Dolphins freebased on the team's charter flights.

By 1984 (when I succeeded Rogin), the editors of SI were convinced that TV sports coverage had become more shilling than substance. The TV and cable networks were in business with the various colleges and leagues, and as a result they had largely abandoned journalism. That provided an opportunity for SI, whose only partners were its readers. The magazine would play a major role as a watchdog in sports, as tenacious at times as that pit bull.

Fans in the state of Oklahoma woke up one day to see the quarterback of their Sooners on the cover of SI—in handcuffs and wearing orange coveralls issued by the department of corrections. They weren't happy. With the magazine, not the quarterback.

Similarly, SI was all over the Pete Rose scandal, breaking numerous cover stories that painstakingly detailed the betting habits and crimes that would eventually send baseball's alltime hits leader to prison and keep him out of the Hall of Fame.

The magazine also had developed a nimbleness that was a far cry from the days when it took six weeks to prepare a cover for press. One Monday afternoon in 1988, SI's editors were celebrating the close of an issue covering the Olympic Games in Seoul. Canadian gold medal sprinter Ben Johnson was on the cover with the single billing: WHOOSH! But then a tip came in from a hockey pal calling from Calgary. He had heard that Johnson flunked his drug test in Seoul. Thought SI might want to check it out.

Frantic calls went out to senior writer Kenny Moore and other SI staffers asleep in Seoul. There were just 12 hours left before the magazine went to press. Three hours later Moore phoned in with the complete story. Names. Places. Drugs. Everything. The cover billing was changed from WHOOSH! to BUSTED!

That kind of good work did not go unnoticed. At decade's end, SI became the first magazine to win back-to-back National Magazine Awards for General Excellence, taking the publishing industry's highest honor in 1989 and '90.

MARK MULVOY *joined SI as a reporter in 1965 and served as managing editor from '84 to '90 and again from '92 to '96.*

1980–1989

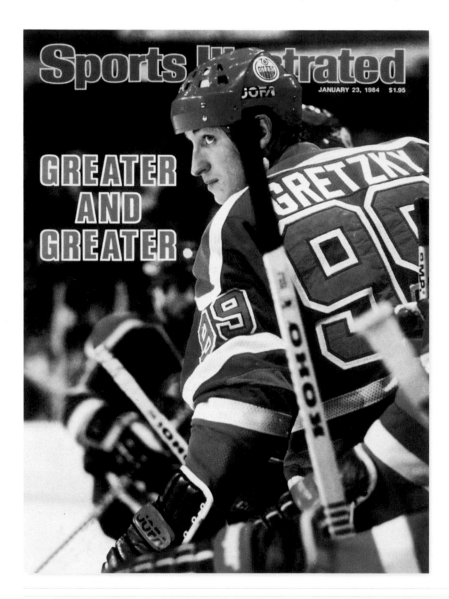

RICKY BELL
January 7, 1980

L.C. GREENWOOD
January 14, 1980

GORDIE HOWE
January 21, 1980

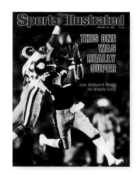

JOHN STALLWORTH
January 28, 1980

CHRISTIE BRINKLEY
February 4, 1980

ERIC HEIDEN
February 11, 1980

MARY DECKER
February 18, 1980

ERIC HEIDEN
February 25, 1980

MIRACLE ON ICE
March 3, 1980

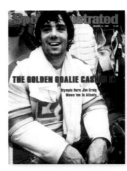

JIM CRAIG
March 10, 1980

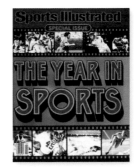

YEAR IN REVIEW
March 17, 1980

ALBERT KING
March 17, 1980

KIRK GIBSON
March 24, 1980

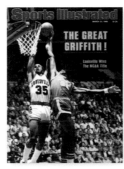

DARRELL GRIFFITH
March 31, 1980

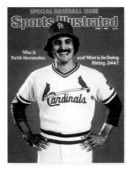

KEITH HERNANDEZ
April 7, 1980

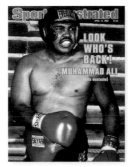

MUHAMMAD ALI
April 14, 1980

SEVE BALLESTEROS
April 21, 1980

ERVING & BIRD
April 28, 1980

KAREEM ABDUL-JABBAR
May 5, 1980

GENUINE RISK
May 12, 1980

ATHLETES & ACADEMICS
May 19, 1980

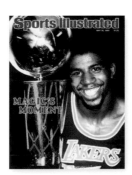

MAGIC JOHNSON
May 26, 1980

> **" SI IS NOT ABOUT** *athletics but about the human spirit. A century from now, when scholars want to learn how Americans lived in our time, they'll turn to* **SPORTS ILLUSTRATED.** *Anyone who wants to know now should do likewise.* **"**
>
> *—The Chicago Tribune, 1984*

JOHNNY RUTHERFORD
June 2, 1980

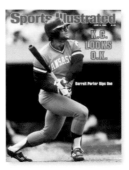

DARRELL PORTER
June 9, 1980

ROBERTO DURAN
June 16, 1980

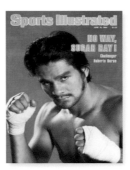

JACK NICKLAUS
June 23, 1980

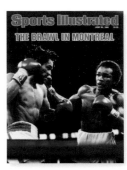

DURAN VS. LEONARD
June 30, 1980

STEVE SCOTT
July 7, 1980

BJORN BORG
July 14, 1980

STEVE CARLTON
July 21, 1980

MOSCOW OLYMPICS
July 28, 1980

REGGIE JACKSON
August 4, 1980

SEBASTIAN COE
August 11, 1980

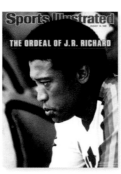

J.R. RICHARD
August 18, 1980

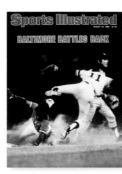

YANKEES VS. ORIOLES
August 25, 1980

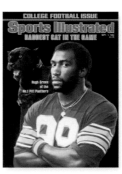

HUGH GREEN
September 1, 1980

NFL PREVIEW
September 8, 1980

JOHN McENROE
September 15, 1980

BILLY SIMS
September 22, 1980

MUHAMMAD ALI
September 29, 1980

GARY CARTER
October 6, 1980

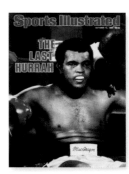

MUHAMMAD ALI
October 13, 1980

PAUL WESTPHAL
October 20, 1980

MIKE SCHMIDT
October 27, 1980

ALBERTO SALAZAR
November 3, 1980

L.C. GREENWOOD
November 10, 1980

HERSCHEL WALKER
November 17, 1980

SUGAR RAY LEONARD
November 24, 1980

COLLEGE BASKETBALL
December 1, 1980

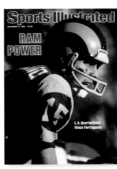

VINCE FERRAGAMO
December 8, 1980

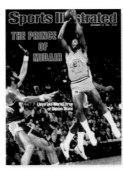

LLOYD FREE
December 15, 1980

OLYMPIC HOCKEY TEAM
December 22, 1980

DAVE WINFIELD
January 5, 1981

CHUCK MUNCIE
January 12, 1980

MARK VAN EEGHEN
January 19, 1981

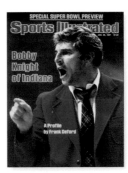

BOBBY KNIGHT
January 26, 1981

ROD MARTIN
February 2, 1981

CHRISTIE BRINKLEY
February 9, 1981

YEAR IN REVIEW
February 12, 1981

BC BETTING SCANDAL
February 16, 1981

BOBBY CARPENTER
February 23, 1981

J.R. RICHARD
March 2, 1981

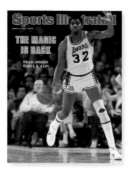

MAGIC JOHNSON
March 9, 1981

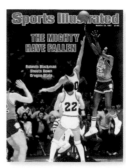

ROLLIE FINGERS
March 16, 1981

ROLANDO BLACKMAN
March 23, 1981

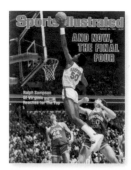

RALPH SAMPSON
March 30, 1981

ISIAH THOMAS
April 6, 1981

SCHMIDT & BRETT
April 13, 1981

TOM WATSON
April 20, 1981

A'S PITCHERS
April 27, 1981

GERRY COONEY
May 4, 1981

CHEEKS & McHALE
May 11, 1981

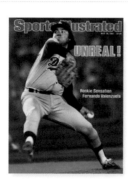

FERNANDO VALENZUELA
May 18, 1981

A.J. FOYT
May 25, 1981

MARVIS & JOE FRAZIER
June 1, 1981

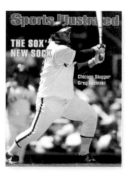

GREG LUZINSKI
June 8, 1981

BJORN BORG
June 15, 1981

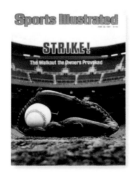

BASEBALL STRIKE
June 22, 1981

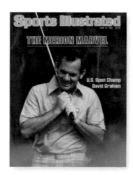

DAVID GRAHAM
June 29, 1981

LEONARD VS. KALULE
July 6, 1981

JOHN McENROE
July 13, 1981

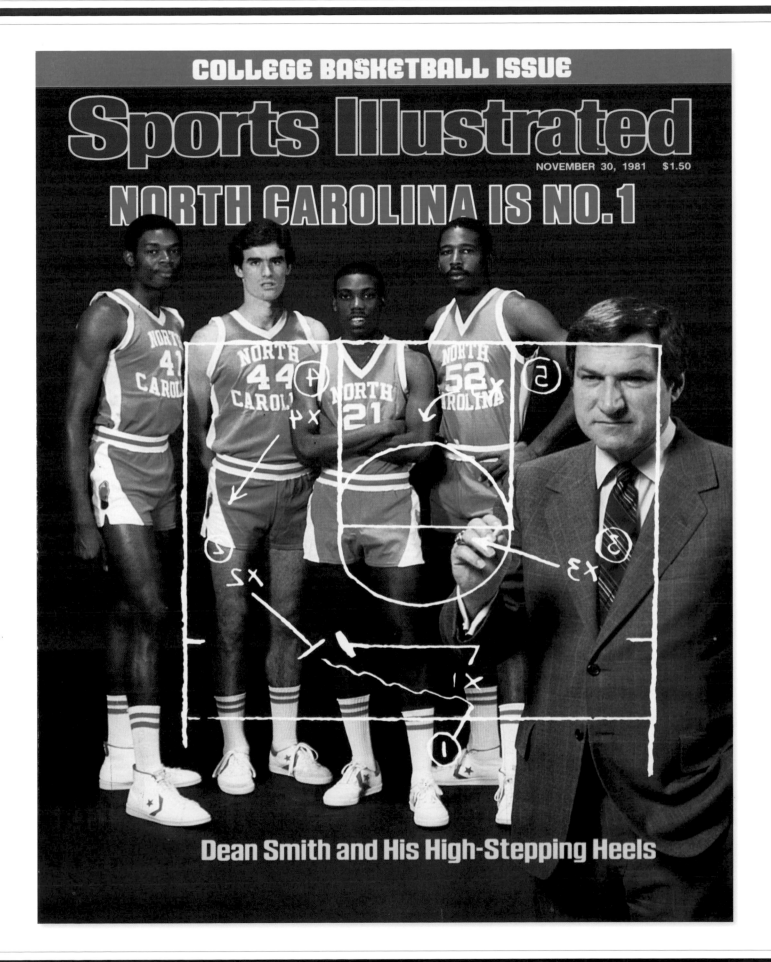

COLLEGE BASKETBALL ISSUE

Sports Illustrated

NOVEMBER 30, 1981 $1.50

NORTH CAROLINA IS NO.1

Dean Smith and His High-Stepping Heels

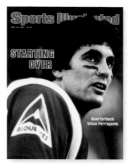

VINCE FERRAGAMO
July 20, 1981

TOM SEAVER
July 27, 1981

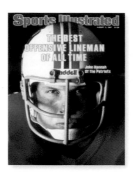

JOHN HANNAH
August 3, 1981

SCHMIDT & BRETT
August 10, 1981

GARY CARTER
August 17, 1981

WENDELL TYLER
August 24, 1981

HERSCHEL WALKER
August 31, 1981

JIM PLUNKETT
September 7, 1981

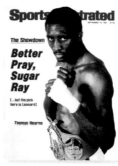

THOMAS HEARNS
September 14, 1981

JOHN McENROE
September 21, 1981

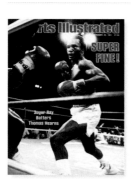

LEONARD VS. HEARNS
September 28, 1981

MARCUS ALLEN
October 5, 1981

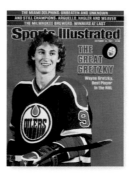

WAYNE GRETZKY
October 12, 1981

TEXAS VS. OKLAHOMA
Ocotber 19, 1981

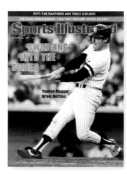

GRAIG NETTLES
October 26, 1981

YANKEES VS. DODGERS
November 2, 1981

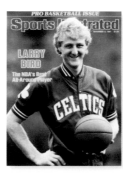

LARRY BIRD
November 9, 1981

HOLMES VS. SNIPES
November 16, 1981

BEAR BRYANT
November 23, 1981

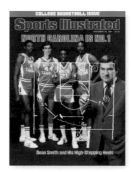

CAROLINA BASKETBALL
November 30, 1981

TONY DORSETT
December 7, 1981

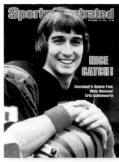

CRIS COLLINSWORTH
December 14, 1981

EARL COOPER
December 21, 1981

SUGAR RAY LEONARD
December 28, 1981

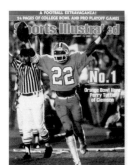

PERRY TUTTLE
January 11, 1982

DWIGHT CLARK
January 18, 1982

JOE MONTANA
January 25, 1982

EARL COOPER
February 1, 1982

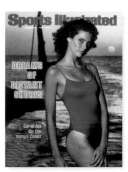

CAROL ALT
February 8, 1982

YEAR IN REVIEW
February 10, 1982

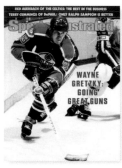

WAYNE GRETZKY
February 15, 1982

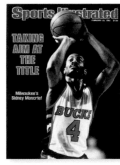

SIDNEY MONCRIEF
February 22, 1982

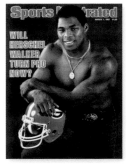

HERSCHEL WALKER
March 1, 1982

BANZAI PIPELINE
March 8, 1982

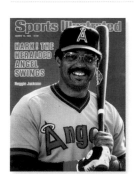

REGGIE JACKSON
March 15, 1982

PATRICK EWING
March 22, 1982

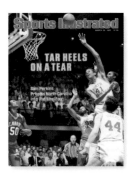

SAM PERKINS
March 29, 1982

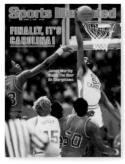

JAMES WORTHY
April 5, 1982

STEVE GARVEY
April 12, 1982

CRAIG STADLER
April 19, 1982

RENALDO NEHEMIAH
April 26, 1982

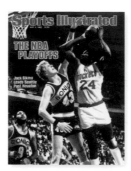

SIKMA & MALONE
May 3, 1982

JONES & FRONTIERE
May 10, 1982

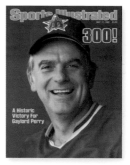

GAYLORD PERRY
May 17, 1982

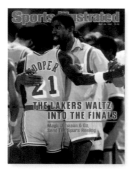

MAGIC JOHNSON
May 24, 1982

JULIUS ERVING
May 31, 1982

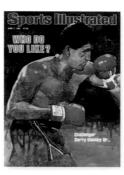

GERRY COONEY
June 7, 1982

COCAINE IN THE NFL
June 14, 1982

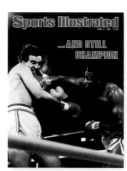

COONEY VS. HOLMES
June 21, 1982

TOM WATSON
June 28, 1982

KENT HRBEK
July 5, 1982

JIMMY CONNORS
July 12, 1982

ROSE & YASTRZEMSKI
July 19, 1982

MARY DECKER
July 26, 1982

RAY MANCINI
August 2, 1982

DALE MURPHY
August 9, 1982

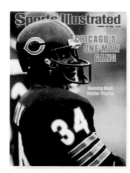

WALTER PAYTON
August 16, 1982

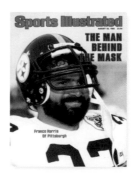

FRANCO HARRIS
August 23, 1982

TOM COUSINEAU
August 30, 1982

FOOTBALL PREVIEW
September 1, 1982

RICKEY HENDERSON
September 6, 1982

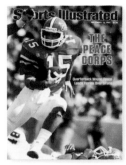

WAYNE PEACE
September 13, 1982

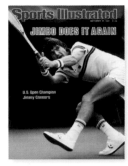

JIMMY CONNORS
September 20, 1982

NFL STRIKE
September 27, 1982

TODD BLACKLEDGE
October 4, 1982

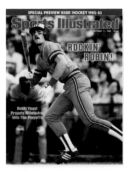

ROBIN YOUNT
October 11, 1982

MARVIN HAGLER
October 18, 1982

CARDS VS. BREWERS
October 25, 1982

MOSES MALONE
November 1, 1982

JOHN ELWAY
November 8, 1982

SUGAR RAY LEONARD
November 15, 1982

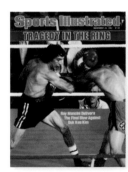

DEATH OF DUK KOO KIM
November 22, 1982

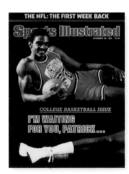

RALPH SAMPSON
November 29, 1982

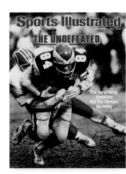

REDSKINS VS. EAGLES
December 6, 1982

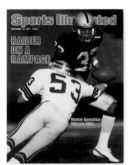

MARCUS ALLEN
December 13, 1982

RALPH SAMPSON
December 20, 1982

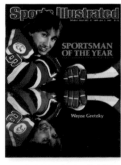

WAYNE GRETZKY
December 27, 1982

GREGG GARRITY
January 10, 1983

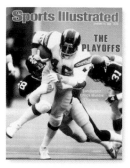

CHUCK MUNCIE
January 17, 1983

ANDRA FRANKLIN
January 24, 1983

DARRYL GRANT
January 31, 1983

JOHN RIGGINS
February 7, 1983

CHERYL TIEGS
February 14, 1983

YEAR IN REVIEW
February 16, 1983

TERRY CUMMINGS
February 21, 1983

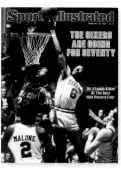

JULIUS ERVING
February 28, 1983

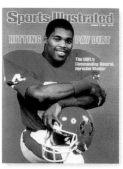

HERSCHEL WALKER
March 7, 1983

PHILADELPHIA PHILLIES
March 14, 1983

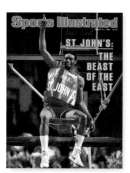

BILLY GOODWIN
March 21, 1983

SPINKS VS. BRAXTON
March 28, 1983

GARY CARTER
April 4, 1983

N.C. STATE'S UPSET
April 11, 1983

TOM SEAVER
April 18, 1983

STEVE GARVEY
April 25, 1983

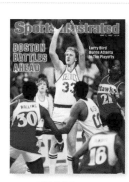

LARRY BIRD
May 2, 1983

KAREEM ABDUL-JABBAR
May 9, 1983

SUNNY'S HALO
May 16, 1983

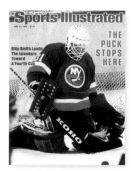

BILLY SMITH
May 23, 1983

LARRY HOLMES
May 30, 1983

MOSES MALONE
June 6, 1983

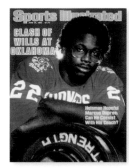

ROD CAREW
June 13, 1983

MARCUS DUPREE
June 20, 1983

DURAN VS. MOORE
June 27, 1983

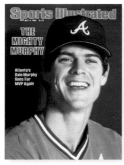

DALE MURPHY
July 4, 1983

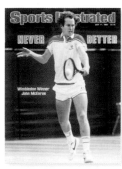

JOHN McENROE
July 11, 1983

DAWSON & STIEB
July 18, 1983

TOM WATSON
July 25, 1983

RICHARD TODD
August 1, 1983

HOWARD COSELL
August 8, 1983

JOHN ELWAY
August 15, 1983

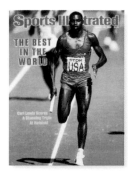

CARL LEWIS
August 22, 1983

TONY DORSETT
August 29, 1983

FOOTBALL PREVIEW
September 1, 1983

MIKE ROZIER
September 5, 1983

EDWIN MOSES
September 12, 1983

MARTINA NAVRATILOVA
September 19, 1983

DOUG FLUTIE
September 26, 1983

STEVE CARLTON
October 3, 1983

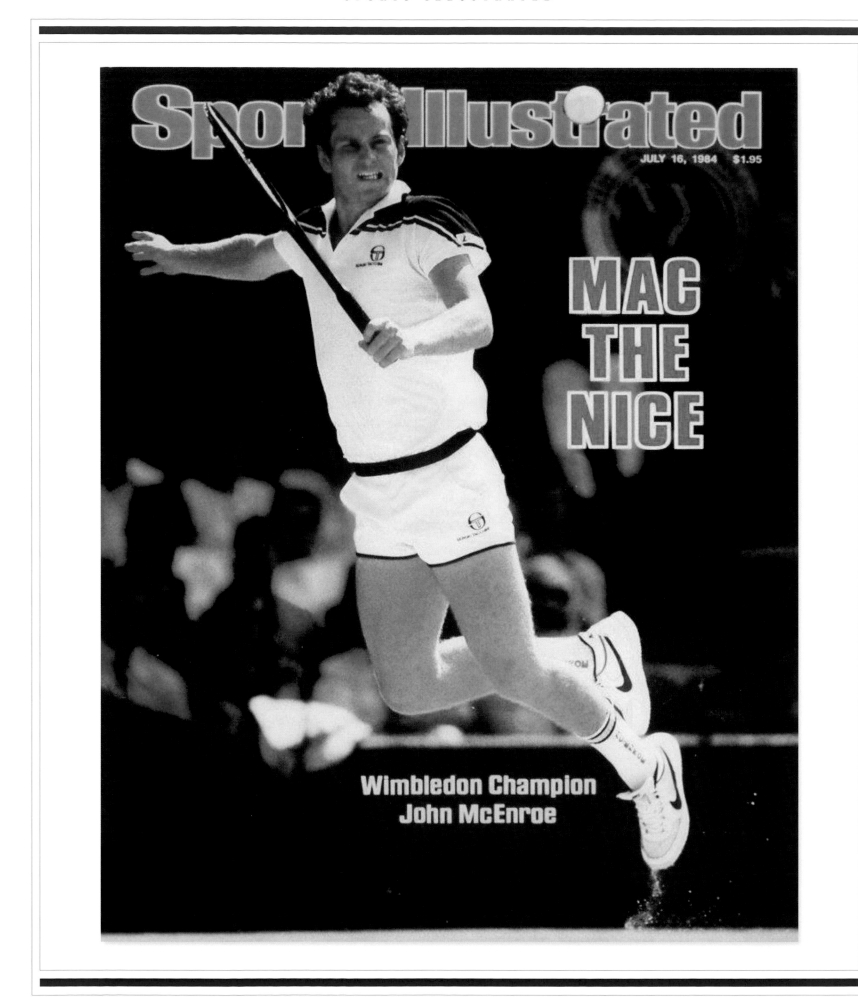

Sports Illustrated

JULY 16, 1984 $1.95

MAC
THE
NICE

Wimbledon Champion
John McEnroe

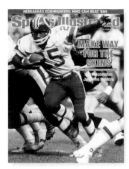

JOE WASHINGTON
October 10, 1983

ERIC DICKERSON
October 17, 1983

RICK DEMPSEY
October 24, 1983

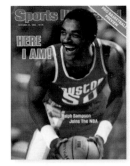

RALPH SAMPSON
October 31, 1983

HAGLER VS. DURAN
November 7, 1983

DAN MARINO
November 14, 1983

HAGLER VS. DURAN
November 21, 1983

JORDAN & PERKINS
November 28, 1983

SAM BOWIE
December 5, 1983

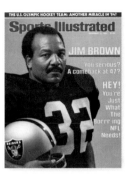

JIM BROWN
December 12, 1983

JOHN RIGGINS
December 19, 1983

MARY DECKER
December 26, 1983

KEITH GRIFFIN
January 9, 1984

JOE THEISMANN
January 16, 1984

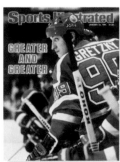

WAYNE GRETZKY
January 23, 1984

JACK SQUIREK
January 30, 1984

OLYMPIC PREVIEW
February 6, 1984

YEAR IN REVIEW
February 8, 1984

PAULINA PORIZKOVA
February 13, 1984

DEBBIE ARMSTRONG
February 20, 1984

BILL JOHNSON
February 27, 1984

MAGIC JOHNSON
March 5, 1984

GEORGE BRETT
March 12, 1984

PATRICK EWING
March 19, 1984

SAM PERKINS
March 26, 1984

YOGI BERRA
April 2, 1984

MICHAEL GRAHAM
April 9, 1984

GOSSAGE & NETTLES
April 16, 1984

DARRYL STRAWBERRY
April 23, 1984

BOB (BULL) SULLIVAN
April 30, 1984

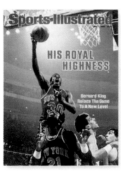

BERNARD KING
May 7, 1984

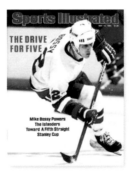

MIKE BOSSY
May 14, 1984

SOVIET BOYCOTT
May 21, 1984

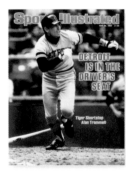

ALAN TRAMMELL
May 28, 1984

MAGIC JOHNSON
June 4, 1984

LEON (BULL) DURHAM
June 11, 1984

MARTINA NAVRATILOVA
June 18, 1984

CARL LEWIS
June 25, 1984

DWIGHT STONES
July 2, 1984

JEFF FLOAT
July 9, 1984

JOHN McENROE
July 16, 1984

OLYMPIC PREVIEW
July 18, 1984

MICHAEL JORDAN
July 23, 1984

JACK LAMBERT
July 30, 1984

RAFER JOHNSON
August 6, 1984

MARY LOU RETTON
August 13, 1984

CARL LEWIS
August 20, 1984

PETE ROSE
August 27, 1984

JOE THEISMANN
September 3, 1984

KOSAR & MARINO
September 5, 1984

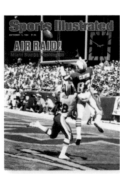

DOLPHINS VS. REDSKINS
September 10, 1984

JOHN McENROE
September 17, 1984

SUTCLIFFE & GOODEN
September 24, 1984

JEFF SMITH
October 1, 1984

SAMMY WINDER
October 8, 1984

WALTER PAYTON
October 15, 1984

ALAN TRAMMELL
October 22, 1984

RUSSELL & BIRD
October 29, 1984

GERRY FAUST
November 5, 1984

HOW TO FIX THE NFL
November 12, 1984

MARK DUPER
November 19, 1984

REAGAN & THE HOYAS
November 26, 1984

DOUG FLUTIE
December 3, 1984

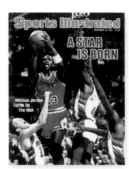

MICHAEL JORDAN
December 10, 1984

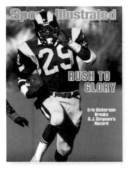

ERIC DICKERSON
December 17, 1984

RETTON & MOSES
December 24, 1984

WALTER ABERCROMBIE
January 7, 1985

DAN MARINO
January 14, 1985

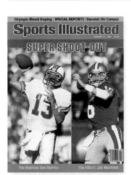

MARINO & MONTANA
January 21, 1985

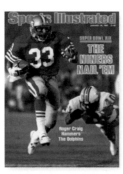

ROGER CRAIG
January 28, 1985

WALTER BERRY
February 4, 1985

PAULINA PORIZKOVA
February 11, 1985

WAYNE GRETZKY
February 18, 1985

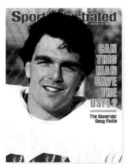

DOUG FLUTIE
February 25, 1985

MIKE SCHMIDT
March 4, 1985

GARY NICKLAUS
March 11, 1985

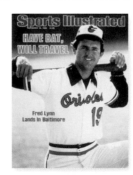

FRED LYNN
March 18, 1985

BASEBALL PARDON
March 25, 1985

FINAL FOUR PREVIEW
April 1, 1985

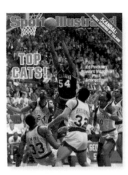

ED PINCKNEY
April 8, 1985

DWIGHT GOODEN
April 15, 1985

HAGLER VS. HEARNS
April 22, 1985

HULK HOGAN
April 29, 1985

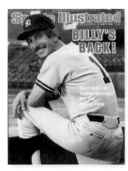

BILLY MARTIN
May 6, 1985

MAGIC JOHNSON
May 13, 1985

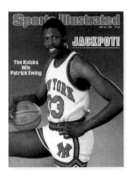

PATRICK EWING
May 20, 1985

HERSCHEL WALKER
May 27, 1985

INDY 500
June 3, 1985

KAREEM ABDUL-JABBAR
June 10, 1985

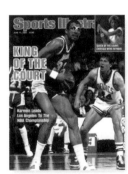

KAREEM ABDUL-JABBAR
June 17, 1985

ANDY NORTH
June 24, 1985

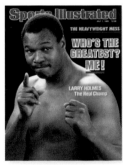

LARRY HOLMES
July 1, 1985

FERNANDO VALENZUELA
July 8, 1985

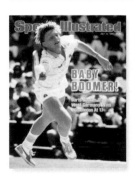

BORIS BECKER
July 15, 1985

HOWIE LONG
July 22, 1985

MARY DECKER SLANEY
July 29, 1985

PEDRO GUERRERO
August 5, 1985

TONY DORSETT
August 12, 1985

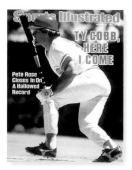

PETE ROSE
August 19, 1985

BERNIE KOSAR
August 26, 1985

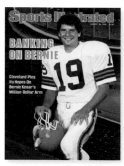

DWIGHT GOODEN
September 2, 1985

FOOTBALL PREVIEW
September 4, 1985

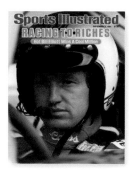

BILL ELLIOTT
September 9, 1985

JOE LOUIS
September 16, 1985

OZZIE SMITH
September 23, 1985

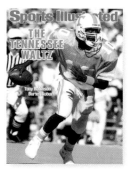

HOLMES VS. SPINKS
September 30, 1985

TONY ROBINSON
October 7, 1985

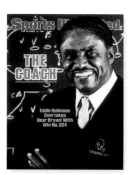

EDDIE ROBINSON
October 14, 1985

JIM McMAHON
October 21, 1985

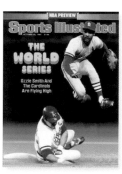

OZZIE SMITH
October 28, 1985

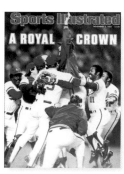

ROYALS WIN SERIES
November 4, 1985

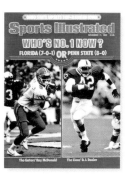

McDONALD & DOZIER
November 11, 1985

DALE BROWN
November 18, 1985

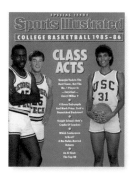

COLLEGE BASKETBALL
November 20, 1985

DANNY WHITE
November 25, 1985

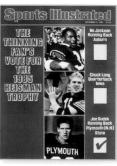

HEISMAN RACE
December 2, 1985

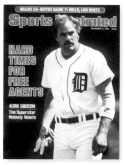

KIRK GIBSON
December 9, 1985

MARCUS ALLEN
December 16, 1985

Sports Illustrated

FEBRUARY 1, 1982 $1.50

SUPER BOWL XVI

THE 49ers
HIT PAY DIRT

Earl Cooper's TD
Jolts the Bengals

KAREEM ABDUL-JABBAR
December 23, 1985

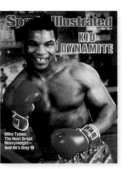

MIKE TYSON
January 6, 1986

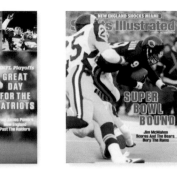

CRAIG JAMES
January 13, 1986

JIM McMAHON
January 20, 1986

MIKE SINGLETARY
January 27, 1986

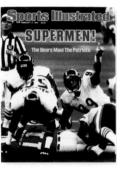

BEARS WIN TITLE
February 3, 1986

ELLE MACPHERSON
February 10, 1986

DANNY MANNING
February 17, 1986

TV SPORTS
February 24, 1986

LARRY BIRD
March 3, 1986

SPORTS GAMBLING
March 10, 1986

MARK ALARIE
March 17, 1986

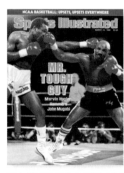

HAGLER VS. MUGABI
March 24, 1986

FINAL FOUR PREVIEW
March 31, 1986

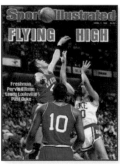

PERVIS ELLISON
April 7, 1986

WADE BOGGS
April 14, 1986

JACK NICKLAUS
April 21, 1986

DOMINIQUE WILKINS
April 28, 1986

A HEMINGWAY STORY
May 5, 1986

ROGER CLEMENS
May 12, 1986

JAMES WORTHY
May 19, 1986

AKEEM OLAJUWON
May 26, 1986

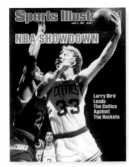

MONTREAL WINS
June 2, 1986

LARRY BIRD
June 9, 1986

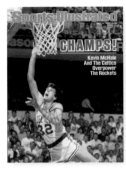

KEVIN McHALE
June 16, 1986

RAY FLOYD
June 23, 1986

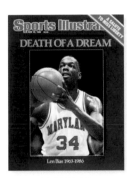

LEN BIAS
June 30, 1986

DIEGO MARADONA
July 7, 1986

BO JACKSON
July 14, 1986

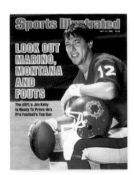

JIM KELLY
July 21, 1986

RICKEY HENDERSON
July 28, 1986

OIL CAN BOYD
August 4, 1986

PERRY & JONES
August 11, 1986

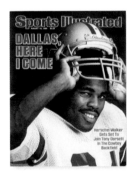

HERSCHEL WALKER
August 18, 1986

RON DARLING
August 25, 1986

KRISTIE PHILLIPS
September 1, 1986

FOOTBALL PREVIEW
September 3, 1986

SUGAR RAY LEONARD
September 8, 1986

IVAN LENDL
September 15, 1986

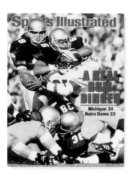

MICHIGAN FOOTBALL
September 22, 1986

TAYLOR & GASTINEAU
September 29, 1986

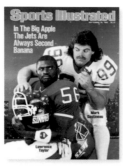

DARRYL STRAWBERRY
October 6, 1986

JOHN ELWAY
October 13, 1986

DeCINCES & GRICH
October 20, 1986

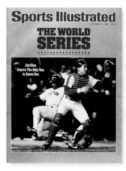

RICE & CARTER
October 27, 1986

RAY KNIGHT
November 3, 1986

NFL INJURY PLAGUE
November 10, 1986

MICHAEL JORDAN
November 17, 1986

DAVID ROBINSON
November 19, 1986

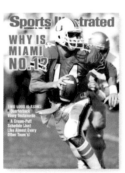

VINNY TESTAVERDE
November 24, 1986

TYSON VS. BERBICK
December 1, 1986

WALTER PAYTON
December 8, 1986

MARK BAVARO
December 15, 1986

JOE PATERNO
December 22, 1986

BRIAN BOSWORTH
January 5, 1987

OZZIE NEWSOME
January 12, 1987

RICH KARLIS
January 19, 1987

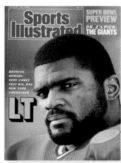

LAWRENCE TAYLOR
January 26, 1987

PHIL SIMMS
February 2, 1987

ELLE MACPHERSON
February 9, 1987

CONNER & REAGAN
February 16, 1987

MAGIC JOHNSON
February 23, 1987

J.R. REID
March 2, 1987

THE RIPKENS
March 9, 1987

VILLANOVA SCANDAL
March 16, 1987

BOBBY KNIGHT
March 23, 1987

HAGLER VS. LEONARD
March 30, 1987

SNYDER & CARTER
April 6, 1987

HAGLER VS. LEONARD
April 13, 1987

BASEBALL SALARIES
April 20, 1987

ROB DEER
April 27, 1987

JULIUS ERVING
May 4, 1987

REGGIE JACKSON
May 11, 1987

ISIAH THOMAS
May 18, 1987

ERIC DAVIS
May 25, 1987

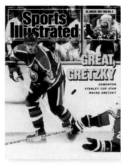

WAYNE GRETZKY
June 1, 1987

LARRY BIRD
June 8, 1987

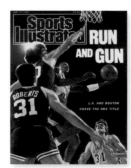

CELTICS VS. LAKERS
June 15, 1987

KAREEM ABDUL–JABBAR
June 22, 1987

SCOTT SIMPSON
June 29, 1987

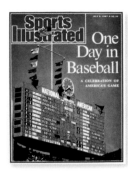

A DAY IN BASEBALL
July 6, 1987

NEW YORK BASEBALL
July 13, 1987

ANDRE DAWSON
July 20, 1987

PIT BULLS
July 27, 1987

VINNY TESTAVERDE
August 3, 1987

TYSON VS. TUCKER
August 10, 1987

ALAN TRAMMELL
August 17, 1987

JIM McMAHON
August 24, 1987

TIM BROWN
August 31, 1987

TOM TRAGER
September 7, 1987

MARK BAVARO
September 9, 1987

JACKIE JOYNER–KERSEE
September 14, 1987

JOHN ELWAY
September 21, 1987

OZZIE SMITH
September 28, 1987

LLOYD MOSEBY
October 5, 1987

STEVE WALSH
October 12, 1987

TWINS VS. TIGERS
October 19, 1987

DAN GLADDEN
October 26, 1987

TWINS WIN SERIES
November 2, 1987

ERIC DICKERSON
November 9, 1987

ROTNEI ANDERSON
November 16, 1987

FENNIS DEMBO
November 18, 1987

DEXTER MANLEY
November 23, 1987

OKLAHOMA FOOTBALL
November 30, 1987

ARNOLD SCHWARZENEGGER
December 7, 1987

BO JACKSON
December 14, 1987

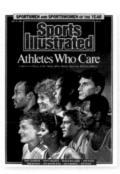

ATHLETES WHO CARE
December 21, 1987

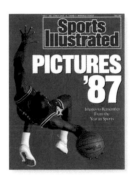

MICHAEL JORDAN
December 28, 1987

MIAMI IS NO. 1
January 11, 1988

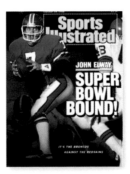

ANTHONY CARTER
January 18, 1988

JOHN ELWAY
January 25, 1988

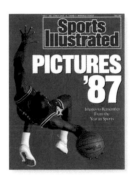

OLYMPIC PREVIEW
January 27, 1988

MIKE TYSON
February 1, 1988

DOUG WILLIAMS
February 8, 1988

ELLE MACPHERSON
February 15, 1988

NBA CENTERS
February 22, 1988

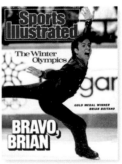

BRIAN BOITANO
February 29, 1988

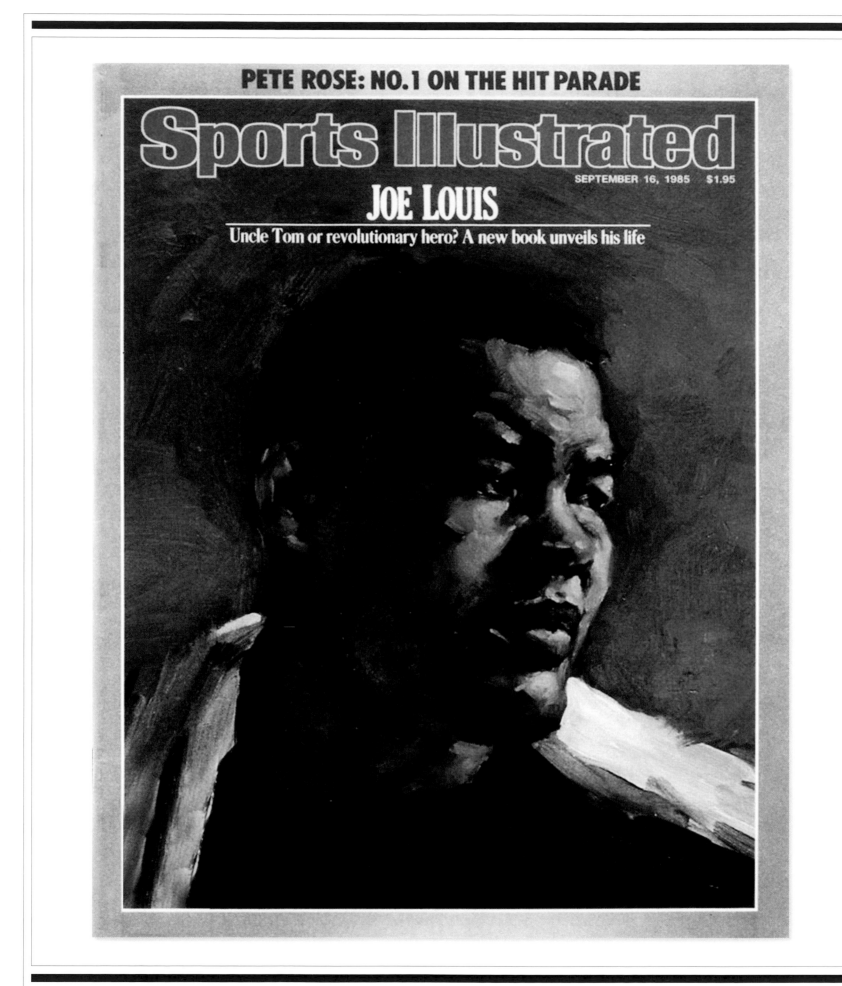

PETE ROSE: NO. 1 ON THE HIT PARADE

Sports Illustrated

SEPTEMBER 16, 1985 $1.95

JOE LOUIS

Uncle Tom or revolutionary hero? A new book unveils his life

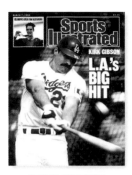
KIRK GIBSON
March 7, 1988

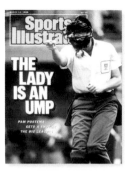
PAM POSTEMA
March 14, 1988

LARRY BIRD
March 21, 1988

MARK MACON
March 28, 1988

CLARK & McGWIRE
April 4, 1988

DANNY MANNING
April 11, 1988

LOS ANGELES LAKERS
April 18, 1988

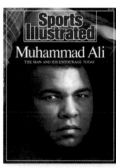
MUHAMMAD ALI
April 25, 1988

BILLY RIPKEN
May 2, 1988

PETE ROSE
May 9, 1988

MICHAEL JORDAN
May 16, 1988

MALONE & MAGIC
May 23, 1988

WAYNE GRETZKY
May 30, 1988

FIRED COACHES
June 6, 1988

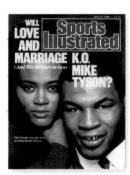
GIVENS & TYSON
June 13, 1988

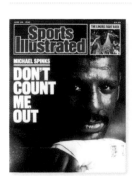
MICHAEL SPINKS
June 20, 1988

MAGIC & LAIMBEER
June 27, 1988

TYSON VS. SPINKS
July 4, 1988

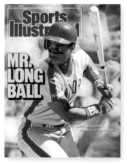
DARRYL STRAWBERRY
July 11, 1988

CASEY AT THE BAT
July 18, 1988

FLORENCE GRIFFITH JOYNER
July 25, 1988

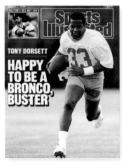

TONY DORSETT
August 1, 1988

BEER
August 8, 1988

SPORTS IN CHINA
August 15, 1988

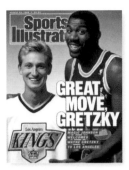

GRETZKY & MAGIC
August 22, 1988

BERNIE KOSAR
August 29, 1988

FOOTBALL PREVIEW
September 5, 1988

JIM McMAHON
September 12, 1988

MATT BIONDI
September 14, 1988

STEFFI GRAF
September 19, 1988

DWIGHT EVANS
September 26, 1988

BEN JOHNSON
October 3, 1988

U.S. SPRINTERS
October 10, 1988

JOSE CANSECO
October 17, 1988

TONY RICE
October 24, 1988

OREL HERSHISER
October 31, 1988

KARL MALONE
November 7, 1988

LANDRY & NOLL
November 14, 1988

NEW ORLEANS SAINTS
November 21, 1988

RODNEY PEETE
November 28, 1988

BILLY OWENS
November 30, 1988

TONY RICE
December 5, 1988

CHARLES BARKLEY
December 12, 1988

OREL HERSHISER
December 19, 1988

FLORENCE GRIFFITH JOYNER
December 26, 1988

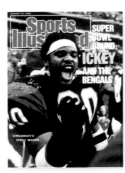

TONY RICE
January 9, 1989

ICKEY WOODS
January 16, 1989

KAREEM ABDUL-JABBAR
January 23, 1989

JERRY RICE
January 30, 1989

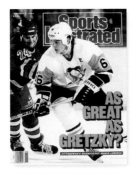

MARIO LEMIEUX
February 6, 1989

KATHY IRELAND
February 7, 1989

PATRICK EWING
February 13, 1989

CHRIS JACKSON
February 20, 1989

OKLAHOMA SCANDAL
February 27, 1989

WADE BOGGS
March 6, 1989

MICHAEL JORDAN
March 13, 1989

JIMMY JOHNSON
March 20, 1989

STEFFI GRAF
March 27, 1989

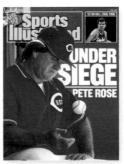

PETE ROSE
April 3, 1988

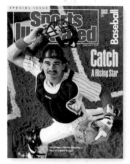

BENITO SANTIAGO
April 5, 1989

ROBINSON & RICE
April 10, 1989

NICK FALDO
April 17, 1989

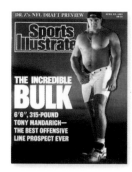

TONY MANDARICH
April 24, 1989

NOLAN RYAN
May 1, 1989

JON PETERS
May 8, 1989

MICHAEL JORDAN
May 15, 1989

JULIE KRONE
May 22, 1989

KENTUCKY SCANDAL
May 29, 1989

JAMES WORTHY
June 5, 1989

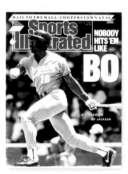

BO JACKSON
June 12, 1989

LEONARD VS. HEARNS II
June 19, 1989

CURTIS STRANGE
June 26, 1989

PETE ROSE
July 3, 1989

RICK REUSCHEL
July 10, 1989

GEORGE FOREMAN
July 17, 1989

BASEBALL BATS
July 24, 1989

GREG LeMOND
July 31, 1989

BOOMER ESIASON
August 7, 1989

MICHAEL JORDAN
August 14, 1989

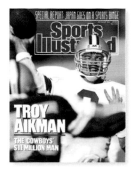

TROY AIKMAN
August 21, 1989

CHRIS EVERT
August 28, 1989

COLLEGE FOOTBALL
September 4, 1989

RANDALL CUNNINGHAM
September 11, 1989

BORIS BECKER
September 18, 1989

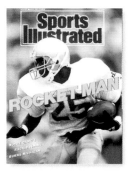

RAGHIB ISMAIL
September 25, 1989

JOE MONTANA
October 2, 1989

STARIKOV & FETISOV
October 9, 1989

RICKEY HENDERSON
October 16, 1989

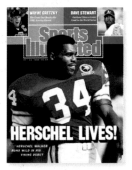

HERSCHEL WALKER
October 23, 1989

EARTHQUAKE SERIES
October 30, 1989

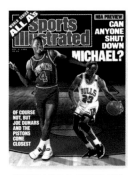

DUMARS & JORDAN
November 6, 1989

DEION SANDERS
November 13, 1989

MUHAMMAD ALI
November 15, 1989

RUMEAL ROBINSON
November 20, 1989

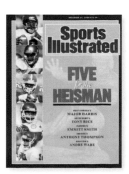

HEISMAN CANDIDATES
November 27, 1989

STEVE McGUIRE
December 4, 1989

LARRY BIRD
December 11, 1989

THE BEST OF THE '80S
December 18, 1989

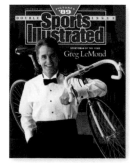

GREG LeMOND
December 25, 1989

The Last Stand

JUNE 8, 1998
www.cnnsi.com

Icons, and Just Plain Cons

BY BILL COLSON

BY THE END OF 1990S, THE balkanization of the American sporting landscape was complete. Thanks to satellite dishes, regional sports networks, single-sport networks and the explosion in talk radio and the Internet, fans had access to a seemingly unlimited supply of programming, statistics, analysis, opinion and predictions. Sure, all 82 Clippers games were available anywhere in the country, but so was just about every USC women's volleyball match . . . or Manchester United soccer game . . . or Big Ten basketball game. And now there were chat rooms and radio call-in shows for a discussion of all of them.

The covers were an integral way for SI to cut through that clutter and reach its audience. For starters, the type became bolder (note the logo change in 1995) and more abundant. In the past, the editors usually billed only the cover story, but increasingly they began to call attention to other pieces inside the magazine. And frequently—in this intensely competitive sports universe—the billings became more pointed. Florida State's football championship in '93 was summed up as a TAINTED TITLE after an investigation revealed that players had gotten improper benefits. WHY THE UNIVERSITY OF MIAMI SHOULD DROP FOOTBALL was the response to that university's scandal-ridden program.

Other covers, like IS TENNIS DYING? and WHO'S COACHING YOUR KID?, initiated a conversation. WHERE'S DADDY? asked another, examining the travesty of athletes fathering multiple children out of wedlock. The national discussion that ensued probed the broader question of fatherhood in society.

The number of sports represented on the cover continued to shrink, with baseball, basketball and football dominating as never before. This was the first decade without a single cover about horse racing; the first in which neither track, swimming, figure skating nor skiing made a cover appearance outside of Olympic coverage; the first with no Indy or Formula One racing cover (though increasingly popular NASCAR did make one appearance).

And the number of athletes deemed cover-worthy also got smaller. In '98, Michael Jordan became the first person to make the cover in three consecutive weeks. All told, of the 514 covers SI produced in the '90s, he was on 35, more than anyone else by far. For one two-year stretch, Tiger Woods was the only golfer to appear on the cover. The '90s featured an extraordinary number of likable and history-making stars—from Cal Ripken Jr. to David Robinson, Peyton Manning, Pete Sampras, John Elway and Derek Jeter—who made it easy to overlook the decade's blemishes. The U.S. women's soccer team was a feel-good story and an empowering one; it also produced perhaps the most memorable cover of the '90s, an exultant Brandi Chastain in her sports bra.

If there were ominous signs of trouble ahead, they were still just suspicions. Not one medal winner in either the two Summer Games or the three Winter Games held during the '90s was caught using performance-enhancing drugs. All three of the Summer Olympics in the decade to come would be riddled with drug scandals.

But if things seemed too good to be true, we were to find out later, they were. The Sammy Sosa–Mark McGwire home-run chase during the summer of '98 generated eight covers. (The Mickey Mantle–Roger Maris race of 1961 generated one.) That year's SPORTSMAN OF THE YEAR cover featured Sosa and McGwire dressed as Greek gods. Barry Bonds would soon exceed their accomplishments. And Alex Rodriguez was setting a pace that threatened to blow away the career home run record. It seemed like a golden age, with nothing more than dietery supplements fueling it.

Not long ago Frank Deford wrote in SI that it took so long to detect how much steroids were contaminating sports because "we were too busy studying the animal entrails of drafts."

True enough, but we were also too busy stargazing.

BILL COLSON *joined* SPORTS ILLUSTRATED *as a reporter in 1978 and was managing editor from 1995 until 2002.*

1990–1999

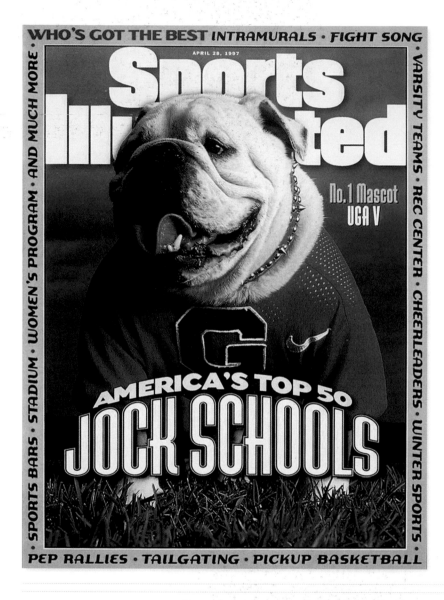

CRAIG ERICKSON
January 8, 1990

JERRY RICE
January 15, 1990

JOHN ELWAY
January 22, 1990

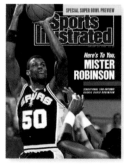

DAVID ROBINSON
January 29, 1990

McINTYRE & MONTANA
February 5, 1990

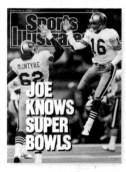

JUDIT MASCO
February 12, 1990

MIKE TYSON
February 19, 1990

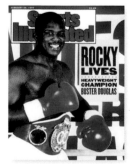

BUSTER DOUGLAS
February 26, 1990

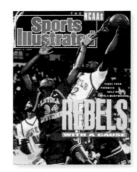

GARY PAYTON
March 5, 1990

TONY LA RUSSA
March 12, 1990

JENNIFER CAPRIATI
March 19, 1990

BO KIMBLE
March 26, 1990

STACEY AUGMON
April 2, 1990

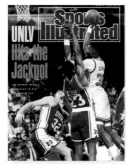

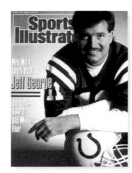

UNLV WINS TITLE
April 9, 1990

TED WILLIAMS
April 16, 1990

TOMAS SANDSTROM
April 23, 1990

JEFF GEORGE
April 30, 1990

KEN GRIFFEY JR.
May 7, 1990

SNEAKER THEFTS
May 14, 1990

MICHAEL JORDAN
May 21, 1990

WILL CLARK
May 28, 1990

LENNY DYKSTRA
June 4, 1990

ISIAH THOMAS
June 11, 1990

> **"SPORTS ILLUSTRATED IS** *the Rolex of magazines. After all these years nobody's topped it. I think it was always a thrill to be on the cover, or be featured in it. I can still remember the headline of the first story they did on me—* **MORE JOAN OF ARC THAN SHIRLEY TEMPLE**—*and I was, like, 15 at the time. It was a big deal, and it still is.***"
>
> —Chris Evert, *1996*

MONICA SELES
June 18, 1990

HALE IRWIN
June 25, 1990

MARVIN HAGLER
July 2, 1990

DARRYL STRAWBERRY
July 9, 1990

MARTINA NAVRATILOVA
July 16, 1990

MINOR LEAGUES
July 23, 1990

GREG LeMOND
July 30, 1990

JOE MONTANA
August 6, 1990

AUTOGRAPH HOUNDS
August 13, 1990

JOSE CANSECO
August 20, 1990

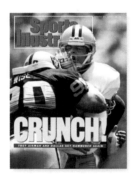

TROY AIKMAN
August 27, 1990

TODD MARINOVICH
September 3, 1990

BARRY SANDERS
September 10, 1990

PETE SAMPRAS
September 17, 1990

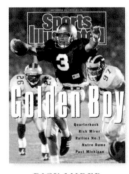

RICK MIRER
September 24, 1990

BOBBY BONILLA
October 1, 1990

O.J. SIMPSON
October 8, 1990

BURT GROSSMAN
October 15, 1990

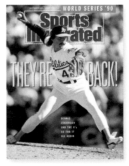

DENNIS ECKERSLEY
October 22, 1990

CHRIS SABO
October 29, 1990

BILL LAIMBEER
November 5, 1990

WILLIAM BELL
November 12, 1990

AUGMON & JOHNSON
November 19, 1990

COLLEGE FOOTBALL
November 26, 1990

MAGIC JOHNSON
December 3, 1990

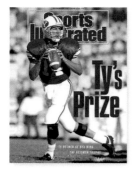

TY DETMER
December 10, 1990

MICHAEL JORDAN
December 17, 1990

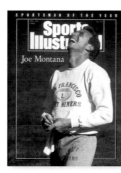

JOE MONTANA
December 24, 1990

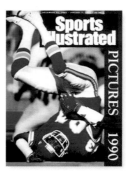

YEAR IN PICTURES
December 31, 1990

DAN MARINO
January 14, 1991

SHAQUILLE O'NEAL
January 21, 1991

OTTIS ANDERSON
January 28, 1991

EVERSON WALLS
February 4, 1991

ASHLEY MONTANA
February 11, 1991

THE DREAM TEAM
February 18, 1991

RAGHIB ISMAIL
February 25, 1991

DARRYL STRAWBERRY
March 4, 1991

ROBERT PARISH
March 11, 1991

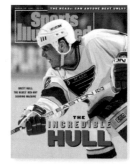

BRETT HULL
March 18, 1991

TYSON VS. RUDDOCK
March 25, 1991

MARK RANDALL
April 1, 1991

GRANT HILL
April 8, 1991

NOLAN RYAN
April 15, 1991

IAN WOOSNAM
April 22, 1991

HOLYFIELD VS. FOREMAN
April 29, 1991

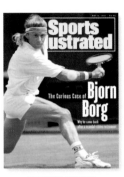

BJORN BORG
May 6, 1991

ROGER CLEMENS
May 13, 1991

MICHAEL JOHNSON
May 20, 1991

MANTLE & MARIS
May 27, 1991

MICHAEL JORDAN
June 3, 1991

MAGIC & JORDAN
June 10, 1991

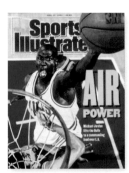

MICHAEL JORDAN
June 17, 1991

MIKE TYSON
June 24, 1991

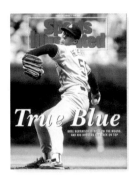

OREL HERSHISER
July 1, 1991

LYLE ALZADO
July 8, 1991

STEFFI GRAF
July 15, 1991

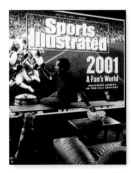

FUTURE OF TV SPORTS
July 22, 1991

CAL RIPKEN JR.
July 29, 1991

THE BLACK ATHLETE
August 5, 1991

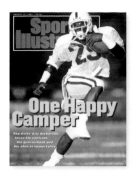

ERIC DICKERSON
August 12, 1991

JOHN DALY
August 19, 1991

DAVID KLINGLER
August 26, 1991

BRUCE SMITH
September 2, 1991

MIKE POWELL
September 9, 1991

JIMMY CONNORS
September 16, 1991

DESMOND HOWARD
September 23, 1991

RAMON MARTINEZ
September 30, 1991

BOBBY HEBERT
October 7, 1991

GARY CLARK
October 14, 1991

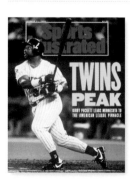

KIRBY PUCKETT
October 21, 1991

GLADDEN & OLSON
October 28, 1991

TWINS WIN SERIES
November 4, 1991

NBA PREVIEW
November 11, 1991

MAGIC JOHNSON
November 18, 1991

CHRISTIAN LAETTNER
November 25, 1991

JIM McMAHON
December 2, 1991

DESMOND HOWARD
December 9, 1991

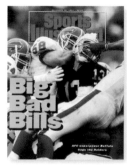

BUFFALO DEFENSE
December 16, 1991

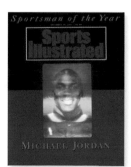

MICHAEL JORDAN
December 23, 1991

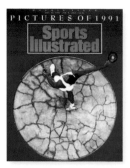

YEAR IN PICTURES
December 30, 1991

MUHAMMAD ALI
January 13, 1992

THURMAN THOMAS
January 20, 1992

A.J. KITT
January 27, 1992

MARK RYPIEN
February 3, 1992

PATRICK EWING
February 10, 1992

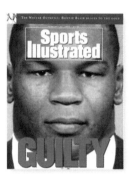

MIKE TYSON
February 17, 1992

BONNIE BLAIR
February 24, 1992

KRISTI YAMAGUCHI
March 2, 1992

KATHY IRELAND
March 9, 1992

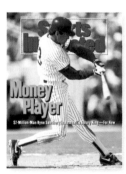

RYNE SANDBERG
March 16, 1992

LARRY BIRD
March 23, 1992

MALCOLM MACKEY
March 30, 1992

KIRBY PUCKETT
April 6, 1992

BOBBY HURLEY
April 13, 1992

FRED COUPLES
April 20, 1992

DEION SANDERS
April 27, 1992

BARRY BONDS
May 4, 1992

DREXLER & JORDAN
May 11, 1992

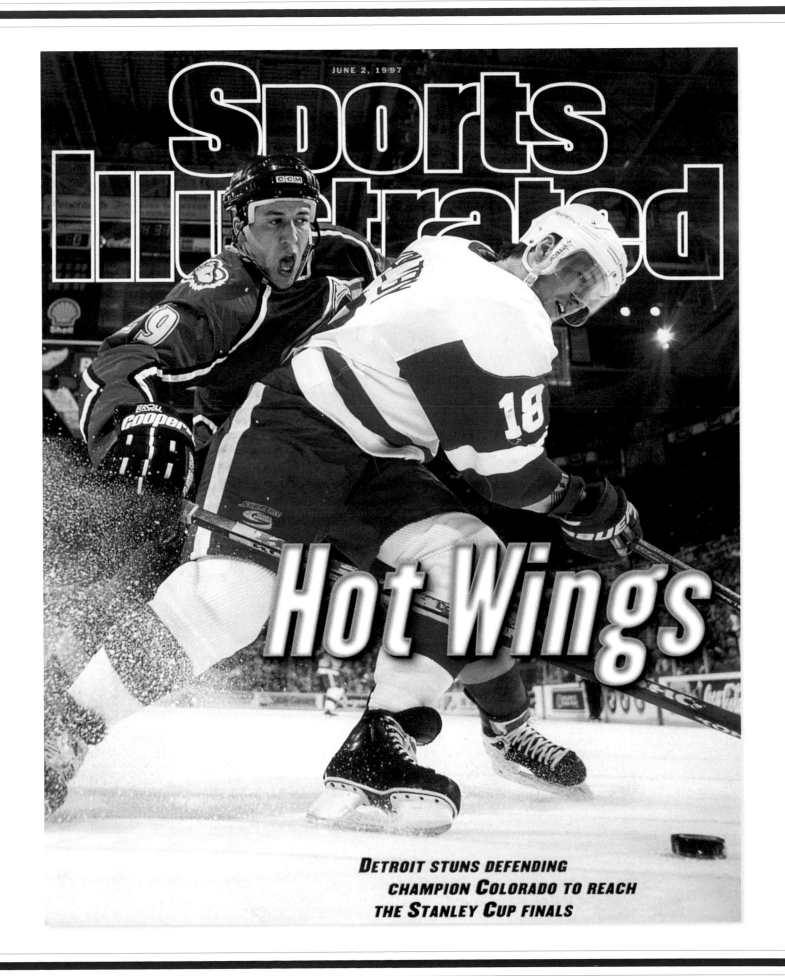

JUNE 2, 1997

Sports Illustrated

Hot Wings

DETROIT STUNS DEFENDING CHAMPION COLORADO TO REACH THE STANLEY CUP FINALS

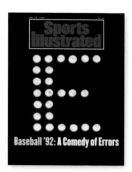

ERRORS EPIDEMIC
May 18, 1992

MICHAEL JORDAN
May 25, 1992

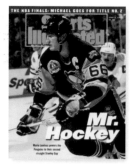

MARK McGWIRE
June 1, 1992

MARIO LEMIEUX
June 8, 1992

MICHAEL JORDAN
June 15, 1992

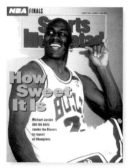

MICHAEL JORDAN
June 22, 1992

TOM KITE
June 29, 1992

STEVE PALERMO
July 6, 1992

ANDRE AGASSI
July 13, 1992

JACKIE JOYNER–KERSEE
July 22, 1992

JOE MONTANA
July 27, 1992

NELSON DIEBEL
August 3, 1992

GAIL DEVERS
August 10, 1992

CARL LEWIS
August 17, 1992

DEION SANDERS
August 24, 1992

COLLEGE FOOTBALL
August 31, 1992

JERRY RICE
September 7, 1992

JIM HARBAUGH
September 14, 1992

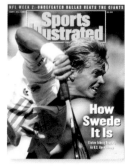

STEFAN EDBERG
September 21, 1992

TONY MANDARICH
September 28, 1992

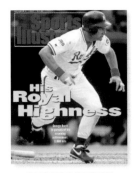

GEORGE BRETT
October 5, 1992

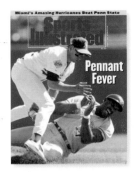

RANDALL CUNNINGHAM
October 12, 1992

A'S VS. BLUE JAYS
October 19, 1992

BRAVES VS. BLUE JAYS
October 26, 1992

TORONTO WINS SERIES
November 2, 1992

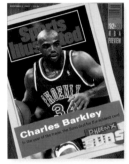

CHARLES BARKLEY
November 9, 1992

DALLAS DEFENSE
November 16, 1992

HOLYFIELD VS. BOWE
November 23, 1992

SHAQUILLE O'NEAL
November 30, 1992

NFL INJURIES
December 7, 1992

LARRY BIRD
December 14, 1992

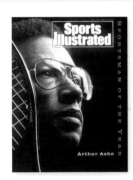

ARTHUR ASHE
December 21, 1992

CARL LEWIS
December 28, 1992

JIM VALVANO
January 11, 1993

STEVE YOUNG
January 18, 1993

EMMITT SMITH
January 25, 1993

SUPER BOWL PREVIEW
February 1, 1993

TROY AIKMAN
February 8, 1993

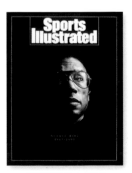

ARTHUR ASHE
February 15, 1993

VENDELA
February 22, 1993

GEORGE STEINBRENNER
March 1, 1993

REESE & EDWARDS
March 8, 1993

REGGIE WHITE
March 15, 1993

DWIGHT GOODEN
March 22, 1993

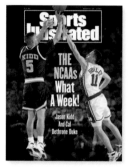

KIDD & HURLEY
March 29, 1993

DAVID CONE
April 5, 1993

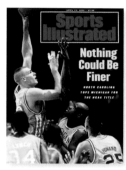

MONTROSS & WEBBER
April 12, 1993

MARIO LEMIEUX
April 19, 1993

JOE MONTANA
April 26, 1993

JOE DiMAGGIO
May 3, 1993

MONICA SELES
May 10, 1993

HAKEEM OLAJUWON
May 17, 1993

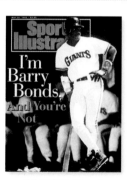

BARRY BONDS
May 24, 1993

PATRICK EWING
May 31, 1993

MICHAEL JORDAN
June 7, 1993

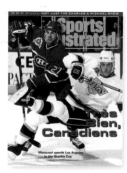

CANADIENS VS. KINGS
June 14, 1993

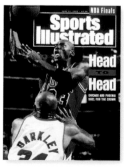

JORDAN & BARKLEY
June 21, 1993

MICHAEL JORDAN
June 28, 1993

MIKE PIAZZA
July 5, 1993

INDIANS TRAGEDY
July 12, 1993

GIBSON & McLAIN
July 19, 1993

GREG NORMAN
July 26, 1993

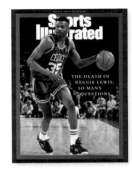

ELWAY & REEVES
August 2, 1993

REGGIE LEWIS
August 9, 1993

PHIL KNIGHT
August 16, 1993

MARY PIERCE
August 23, 1993

SCOTT BENTLEY
August 30, 1993

JUNIOR SEAU
September 6, 1993

JOE MONTANA
September 13, 1993

WHITAKER VS. CHAVEZ
September 20, 1993

RON GANT
September 27, 1993

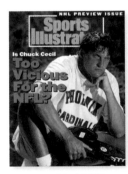

BOOMER ESIASON
October 4, 1993

CHUCK CECIL
October 11, 1993

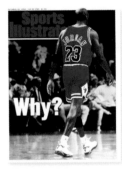

MICHAEL JORDAN
October 18, 1993

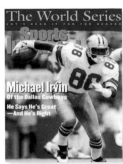

MICHAEL IRVIN
October 25, 1993

JOE CARTER
November 1, 1993

MOURNING & RUSSELL
November 8, 1993

HOLYFIELD VS. BOWE II
November 15, 1993

JIM FLANIGAN
November 22, 1993

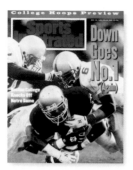

BC VS. NOTRE DAME
November 29, 1993

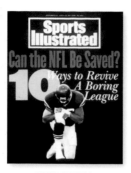

NFL WOES
December 6, 1993

DAMON BAILEY
December 13, 1993

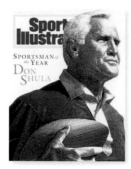

DON SHULA
December 20, 1993

YEAR IN REVIEW
December 27, 1993

FLORIDA STATE
January 10, 1994

NANCY KERRIGAN
January 17, 1994

JOE MONTANA
January 24, 1994

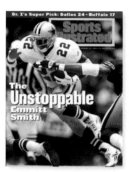

EMMITT SMITH
January 31, 1994

EMMITT SMITH
February 7, 1994

THE DREAM TEAM
February 14, 1994

TOMMY MOE
February 21, 1994

JANSEN & BLAIR
February 28, 1994

DAVID ROBINSON
March 7, 1994

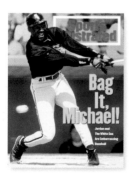

MICHAEL JORDAN
March 14, 1994

BILL CLINTON
March 21, 1994

BILL CURLEY
March 28, 1994

KEN GRIFFEY JR.
April 4, 1994

CORLISS WILLIAMSON
April 11, 1994

MICKEY MANTLE
April 18, 1994

DAN WILKINSON
April 25, 1994

GARY PAYTON
May 2, 1994

TENNIS IN TROUBLE
May 9, 1994

FLORIDA STATE SCANDAL
May 16, 1994

BASEBALL BRAWLS
May 23, 1994

JOHN STARKS
May 30, 1994

KEN GRIFFEY JR.
June 6, 1994

MARK MESSIER
June 13, 1994

RICHTER & EWING
June 20, 1994

O.J. SIMPSON
June 27, 1994

ERNIE STEWART
July 4, 1994

PETE SAMPRAS
July 11, 1994

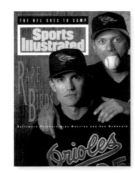

MUSSINA & McDONALD
July 18, 1994

WORLD CUP
July 25, 1994

SWITZER'S COWBOYS
August 1, 1994

THOMAS & GRIFFEY
August 8, 1994

40TH ANNIVERSARY
August 15, 1994

BASEBALL STRIKE
August 22, 1994

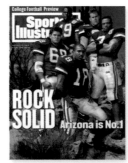

ARIZONA FOOTBALL
August 29, 1994

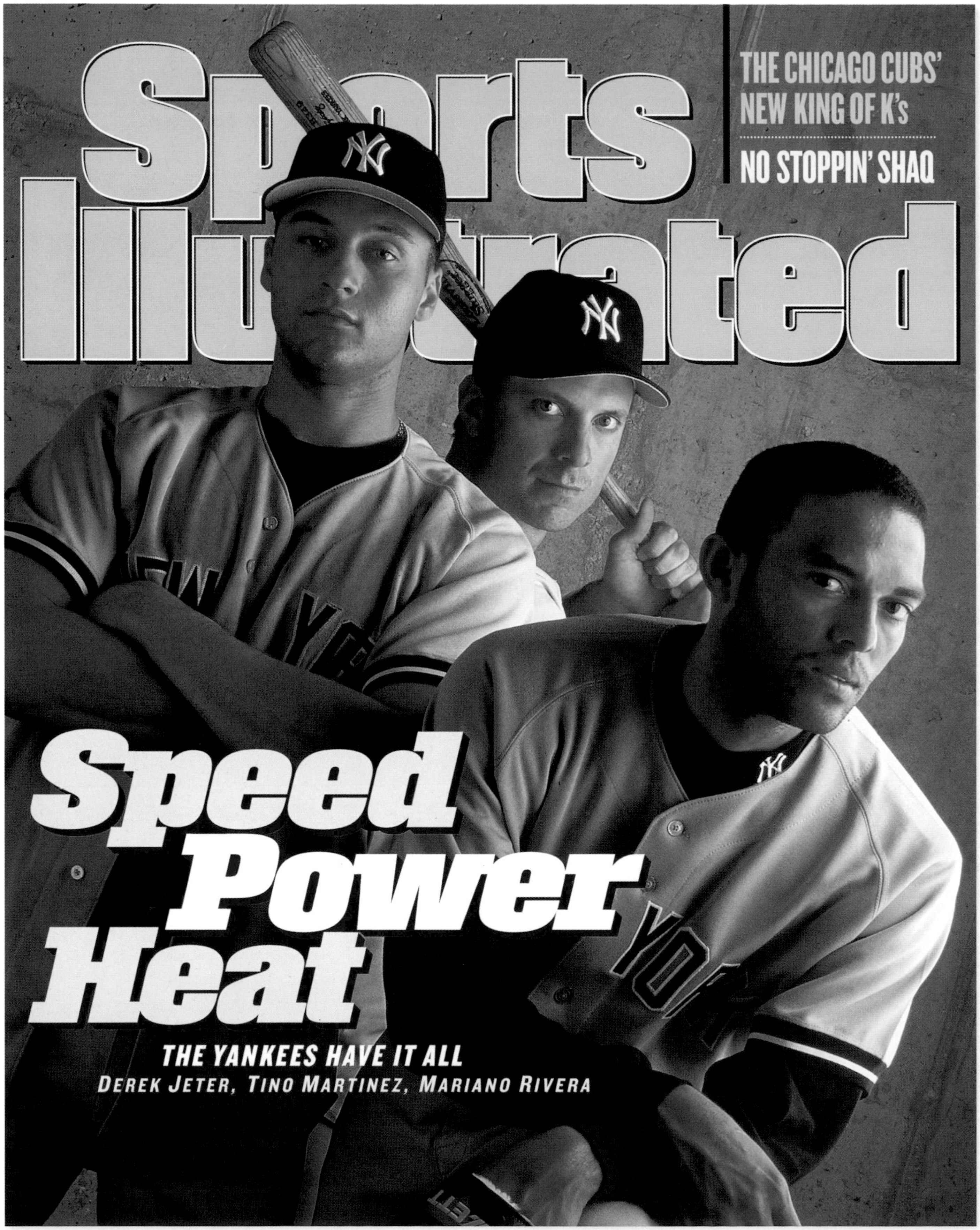

Sports Illustrated

THE CHICAGO CUBS'
NEW KING OF K's

NO STOPPIN' SHAQ

Speed Power Heat

THE YANKEES HAVE IT ALL
DEREK JETER, TINO MARTINEZ, MARIANO RIVERA

WILL WOLFORD
September 5, 1994

DAN MARINO
September 12, 1994

40TH ANNIVERSARY
September 19, 1994

STEVE McNAIR
September 26, 1994

PERNELL WHITAKER
October 10, 1994

NATRONE MEANS
October 17, 1994

FREDDIE SCOTT
October 24, 1994

JAPAN'S WORLD SERIES
October 31, 1994

HORACE GRANT
November 7, 1994

FOREMAN VS. MOORER
November 14, 1994

RICKY WATTERS
November 21, 1994

FELIPE LOPEZ
November 28, 1994

PITTSBURGH STEELERS
December 5, 1994

DALLAS COWBOYS
December 12, 1994

BLAIR & KOSS
December 19, 1994

JERRY RICE
December 26, 1994

TOM OSBORNE
January 9, 1995

YOUNG & AIKMAN
January 16, 1995

Also, the image for MICHAEL WESTBROOK:

MICHAEL WESTBROOK
October 3, 1994

STEVE YOUNG
January 23, 1995

DERRICK COLEMAN
January 30, 1995

STEVE YOUNG
February 6, 1995

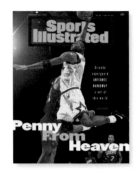

ANFERNEE HARDAWAY
February 13, 1995

DANIELA PESTOVA
February 20, 1995

STRAWBERRY & GOODEN
February 27, 1995

JERRY STACKHOUSE
March 6, 1995

ANDRE AGASSI
March 13, 1995

MICHAEL JORDAN
March 20, 1995

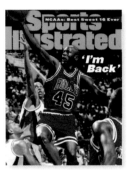

MICHAEL JORDAN
March 27, 1995

COREY BECK
April 3, 1995

ED O'BANNON
April 10, 1995

BEN CRENSHAW
April 17, 1995

THE MONTANAS
April 24, 1995

CAL RIPKEN JR.
May 1, 1995

VLADE DIVAC
May 8, 1995

COACHES IN TROUBLE
May 15, 1995

O'NEAL VS. JORDAN
May 22, 1995

DENNIS RODMAN
May 29, 1995

MATT WILLIAMS
June 5, 1995

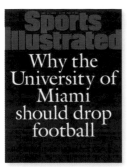

MIAMI FOOTBALL
June 12, 1995

CLYDE DREXLER
June 19, 1995

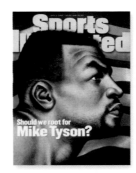

KEVIN GARNETT
June 26, 1995

MIKE TYSON
July 3, 1995

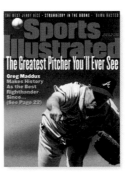

HIDEO NOMO
July 10, 1995

MONICA SELES
July 17, 1995

NASCAR
July 24, 1995

JOHN DALY
July 31, 1995

CAL RIPKEN JR.
August 7, 1995

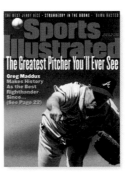

GREG MADDUX
August 14, 1995

MICKEY MANTLE
August 21, 1995

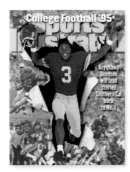

KEYSHAWN JOHNSON
August 28, 1995

DAN MARINO
September 4, 1995

CAL RIPKEN JR.
September 11, 1995

EMMITT SMITH
September 18, 1995

DANNY WUERFFEL
September 25, 1995

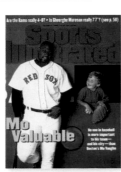

MO VAUGHN
October 2, 1995

DEION SANDERS
October 9, 1995

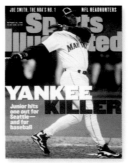

KEN GRIFFEY JR.
October 16, 1995

RODMAN & JORDAN
October 23, 1995

BO JACKSON
October 30, 1995

BRAVES WIN SERIES
November 6, 1995

DARNELL AUTRY
November 13, 1995

ELVIS GRBAC
November 20, 1995

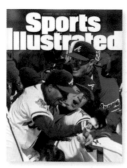

JACQUE VAUGHN
November 27, 1995

ART MODELL
December 4, 1995

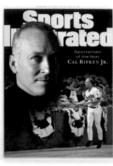

RILEY & SHULA
December 11, 1995

CAL RIPKEN JR.
December 18, 1995

STEVE TASKER
December 25, 1995

BILLY PAYNE
January 8, 1996

BRETT FAVRE
January 15, 1996

EMMITT SMITH
January 22, 1996

MAZZA & BANKS
January 29, 1996

EMMITT SMITH
February 5, 1996

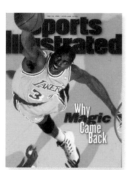

MAGIC JOHNSON
February 12, 1996

MARCUS STROUD
February 19, 1996

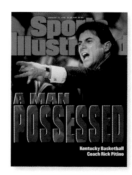

RICK PITINO
February 26, 1996

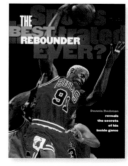

DENNIS RODMAN
March 4, 1996

O'DONNELL & GRETZKY
March 11, 1996

JAY BUHNER
March 18, 1996

DARVIN HAM
March 25, 1996

MANNY RAMIREZ
April 1, 1996

ANTOINE WALKER
April 8, 1996

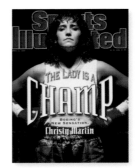

CHRISTY MARTIN
April 15, 1996

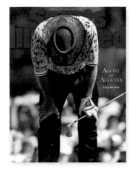

GREG NORMAN
April 22, 1996

DAVID ROBINSON
April 29, 1996

ALBERT BELLE
May 6, 1996

MARINO & JOHNSON
May 13, 1996

MARGE SCHOTT
May 20, 1996

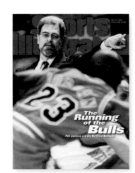

PHIL JACKSON
May 27, 1996

MICHAEL JORDAN
June 3, 1996

GARY PAYTON
June 10, 1996

MICHAEL JORDAN
June 17, 1996

RICHIE PARKER
June 24, 1996

EMMITT SMITH
July 1, 1996

ALEX RODRIGUEZ
July 8, 1996

DREW ROSENHAUS
July 15, 1996

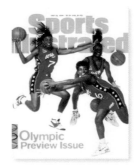

OLYMPIC PREVIEW
July 22, 1996

TOM DOLAN
July 29, 1996

CARL LEWIS
August 5, 1996

MICHAEL JOHNSON
August 12, 1996

AL SIMMONS
August 19, 1996

THE MANNINGS
August 26, 1996

NFL PREVIEW
September 2, 1996

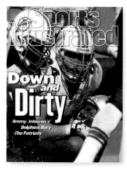

MIAMI DOLPHINS
September 9, 1996

AHMAN GREEN
September 16, 1996

RON POWLUS
September 23, 1996

ALI & FRAZIER
September 30, 1996

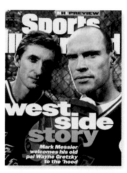

GRETZKY & MESSIER
October 7, 1996

ROBERTO ALOMAR
Ocotber 14, 1996

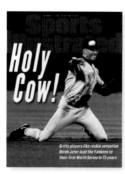

DEREK JETER
October 21, 1996

TIGER WOODS
October 28, 1996

YANKEES WIN SERIES
November 4, 1996

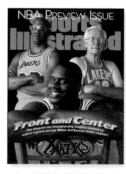

LAKERS CENTERS
November 11, 1996

HOLYFIELD VS. TYSON
November 18, 1996

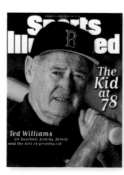

TED WILLIAMS
November 25, 1996

DANNY FORTSON
December 2, 1996

WARRICK DUNN
December 9, 1996

BRETT FAVRE
December 16, 1996

TIGER WOODS
December 23, 1996

JOHN ELWAY
December 30, 1996

BRUNELL & COLLINS
January 13, 1997

ANTONIO FREEMAN
January 20, 1997

FAVRE & HOLMGREN
January 27, 1997

DESMOND HOWARD
February 3, 1997

TERRELL BRANDON
February 10, 1997

KEYS TO NFL SUCCESS
February 17, 1997

TYRA BANKS
February 21, 1997

RODRIGUEZ & JETER
February 24, 1997

SUGAR RAY LEONARD
March 3, 1997

MICHAEL JORDAN
March 10, 1997

THE WIDEMANS
March 17, 1997

SCOT POLLARD
March 24, 1997

RANDY JOHNSON
March 31, 1997

MILES SIMON
April 7, 1997

DRUGS IN SPORTS
April 14, 1997

TIGER WOODS
April 21, 1997

TOP SPORTS SCHOOLS
April 28, 1997

JACKIE ROBINSON
May 5, 1997

KARL MALONE
May 12, 1997

SMITH & JORDAN
May 19, 1997

DEION SANDERS
May 26, 1997

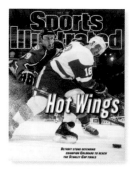

KIRK MALTBY
June 2, 1997

MICHAEL JORDAN
June 9, 1997

KARL MALONE
June 16, 1997

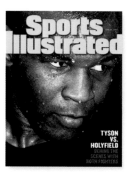

MICHAEL JORDAN
June 23, 1997

MIKE TYSON
June 30, 1997

TYSON VS. HOLYFIELD II
July 7, 1997

PETE SAMPRAS
July 14, 1997

FRANK GIFFORD
July 21, 1997

TONY GWYNN
July 28, 1997

STEVE YOUNG
August 4, 1997

IVAN RODRIGUEZ
August 11, 1997

BOOGER SMITH
August 18, 1997

JOE JUREVICIUS
August 25, 1997

AFC CENTRAL QBS
September 1, 1997

STEVE YOUNG
September 8, 1997

VENUS WILLIAMS
September 15, 1997

PEYTON MANNING
September 22, 1997

WARRICK DUNN
September 29, 1997

TIGER WOODS
October 6, 1997

EMMITT SMITH
October 13, 1997

KEVIN FAULK
October 20, 1997

LARRY BIRD
October 27, 1997

MARLINS WIN SERIES
November 3, 1997

GRANT HILL
November 10, 1997

STEVE WOJCIECHOWSKI
November 17, 1997

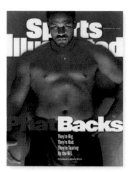

JEROME BETTIS
November 24, 1997

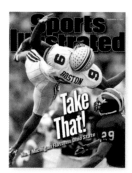

MICHIGAN FOOTBALL
December 1, 1997

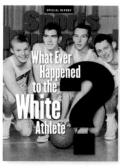

THE WHITE ATHLETE
December 8, 1997

LATRELL SPREWELL
December 15, 1997

DEAN SMITH
December 22, 1997

EVANDER HOLYFIELD
December 29, 1997

MICHIGAN FOOTBALL

BRENT JONES
January 12, 1998

ANTONIO FREEMAN
January 19, 1998

ONLINE GAMBLING
January 26, 1998

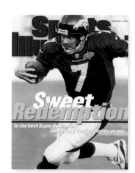

JOHN ELWAY
February 2, 1998

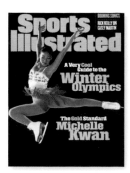

MICHELLE KWAN
February 9, 1998

MICHAEL JORDAN
February 16, 1998

HEIDI KLUM
February 20, 1998

HERMANN MAIER
February 27, 1998

PAT SUMMITT
March 2, 1998

ALLEN IVERSON
March 9, 1998

RICKY MOORE
March 16, 1998

MARK McGWIRE
March 23, 1998

NAZR MOHAMMED
March 30, 1998

WAYNE TURNER
April 6, 1998

TIGER WOODS
April 13, 1998

PEDRO MARTINEZ
April 20, 1998

MAGIC & KOBE
April 27, 1998

PATERNITY SUITS
May 4, 1998

CHICAGO BULLS
May 11, 1998

NEW YORK YANKEES
May 18, 1998

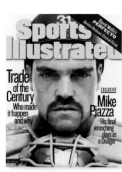

MIKE PIAZZA
May 25, 1998

JOHN STOCKTON
June 1, 1998

PIPPEN & JORDAN
June 8, 1998

MICHAEL JORDAN
June 15, 1998

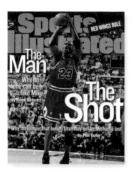

MICHAEL JORDAN
June 22, 1998

SAMMY SOSA
June 29, 1998

ALEX RODRIGUEZ
July 6, 1998

BINGHAM & ALI
July 13, 1998

MIKE DITKA
July 20, 1998

MARK O'MEARA
July 27, 1998

MARK McGWIRE
August 3, 1998

RANDY JOHNSON
August 10, 1998

BRETT FAVRE
August 17, 1998

BABE RUTH
August 24, 1998

ANDY KATZENMOYER
August 31, 1998

MARK McGWIRE
September 7, 1998

MARK McGWIRE
September 14, 1998

SAMMY SOSA
September 21, 1998

TERRELL DAVIS
September 28, 1998

MARK McGWIRE
October 5, 1998

SHANE SPENCER
October 12, 1998

UMPS UNDER FIRE
October 19, 1998

KEVIN GOGAN
October 26, 1998

YANKEES WIN SERIES
November 2, 1998

DOUG FLUTIE
November 9, 1998

RICKY WILLIAMS
November 16, 1998

ARTHUR LEE
November 23, 1998

JOHN ELWAY
November 30, 1998

RANDALL CUNNINGHAM
December 7, 1998

BILL PARCELLS
December 14, 1998

McGWIRE & SOSA
December 21, 1998

TOP YEARS IN SPORTS
December 26, 1998

PEERLESS PRICE
January 11, 1999

KEYSHAWN JOHNSON
January 18, 1999

MICHAEL JORDAN
January 25, 1999

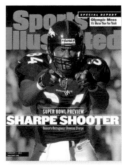

SHANNON SHARPE
February 1, 1999

JOHN ELWAY
February 8, 1999

REBECCA ROMIJN
February 12, 1999

SCOTTIE PIPPEN
February 15, 1999

ELTON BRAND
February 22, 1999

ROGER CLEMENS
March 1, 1999

DENNIS RODMAN
March 8, 1999

MATEEN CLEAVES
March 15, 1999

WALLY SZCZERBIAK
March 22, 1999

KEVIN BROWN
March 29, 1999

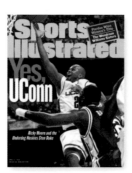

RICKY MOORE
April 5, 1999

DAVID DUVAL
April 12, 1999

COUCH & SMITH
April 19, 1999

WAYNE GRETZKY
April 26, 1999

KEVIN GARNETT
May 3, 1999

BILL RUSSELL
May 10, 1999

KEN GRIFFEY JR.
May 17, 1999

ICE CUBE & SHAQ
May 24, 1999

TIM DUNCAN
May 31, 1999

LATRELL SPREWELL
June 7, 1999

ANDRE AGASSI
June 14, 1999

DEREK JETER
June 21, 1999

SPURS VS. KNICKS
June 28, 1999

DAVID ROBINSON
July 5, 1999

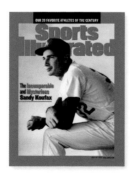

SANDY KOUFAX
July 12, 1999

BRANDI CHASTAIN
July 19, 1999

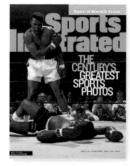

ALI & LISTON
July 26, 1999

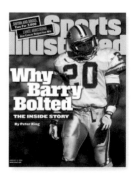

BARRY SANDERS
August 9, 1999

LAVAR ARRINGTON
August 16. 1999

TIGER WOODS
August 23, 1999

WILLIAMS & BROWN
August 30, 1999

METS INFIELD
September 6, 1999

PEDOPHILE COACHES
September 13, 1999

SERENA WILLIAMS
September 20, 1999

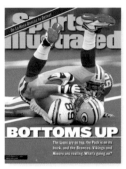

MARK CHMURA
September 27, 1999

JUSTIN LEONARD
October 4, 1999

TERRELL DAVIS
October 11, 1999

KURT WARNER
October 18, 1999

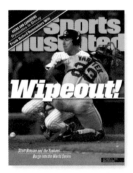

BROSIUS & VARITEK
October 25, 1999

PHIL JACKSON
November 1, 1999

WALTER PAYTON
November 8, 1999

CHRIS PORTER
November 15, 1999

PEYTON MANNING
November 22, 1999

20TH CENTURY SPORTS
November 29, 1999

ANDRE DAVIS
December 6, 1999

DAN MARINO
December 13, 1999

U.S. SOCCER TEAM
December 20, 1999

BEST PLAYERS BY STATE
December 27, 1999

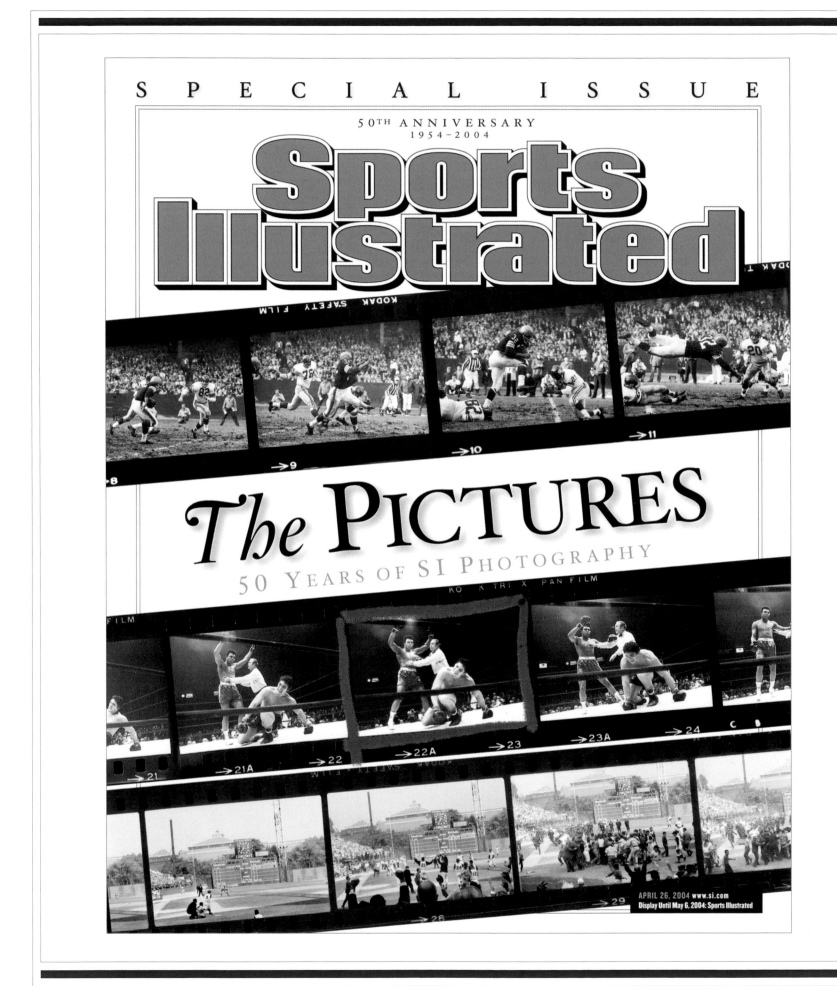

On the Shoulders of Giants

BY TERRY McDONELL

COVERS START WITH IDEAS but succeed only in execution. And that execution is always collaborative, usually between the editor, art director and director of photography. Their titles have changed over the years—art directors became creative directors, photo editors became directors of photography—but the job hasn't. Making the cover can be the most challenging and satisfying work at the magazine each week, and while it is the editor's call, the credit for a successful cover is far from his alone.

In its 56-year history, SPORTS ILLUSTRATED has been art directed by only six men. The first, the whimsical Jerome Snyder, was a traditional illustrator as well as a graphic designer, and his covers were a reflection of a "leisure time" aesthetic that was then prevalent in all aspects of American life. Following Snyder was Dick Gangel, the elegant and intuitive former WWII pilot who arrived from LIFE in 1960. The collaboration between Gangel and managing editor Andre Laguerre redefined American magazine journalism, and by the time Gangel retired, in 1981, SI had emerged as a graphically sophisticated mass-audience magazine with covers that enjoyed status, influence and even an emerging Jinx mythology. The aesthetic was both bold and nuanced.

Harvey Grut had the job in 1983 when SI became the first all-color national weekly magazine. Grut had joined the magazine in 1953, before its debut, as what was then known as a cutter-paster. Rick Warner carried on when Grut retired in 1984, and he was succeeded two years later by Steve Hoffman, whose tenure lasted longer even than that of the great Gangel. Hoffman rethought and redesigned SI's cover many times over his 23 years, basically reinventing it with a modernism that continues to serve the magazine.

The work of the 10 photo editors who have worked at SI since 1954 is dominated by three—Gerald Astor who was originally a staff writer before taking over the photo department, for which he hired or developed some of SI's top shooters, including Walter Iooss Jr., Neil Leifer and John Zimmerman; Heinz Kluetmeier, who is a gifted shooter himself; and Steve Fine, who came to SI from *The New York Times* in 1992 and whose assignments have dominated since he became the top picture editor in 1996. Under Fine, SI's cover photography has been built on unique event coverage by staff photographers (Robert Beck, John Biever, John McDonough and Al Tielemans, among them) combining peak action with a sense of place and emotion ("tears and cheers," as it's referred to at SI), while cover portraits by Iooss, Gerard Rancinan and Michael O'Neill have drilled into the core of sports personalities.

Fine's photographs along with Hoffman's shrewd and sharply graphic typography made for covers with increasingly bolder headlines and a cleaner design. (Hoffman also brought in new and more sophisticated typefaces—with sporting names like Knockout, Fenway and Wrigley—throughout the magazine.)

In 2009 Hoffman retired from SI to concentrate on more eclectic design work (like this book, for example), and his deputy, Chris Hercik, took over the art direction. He has taken his mantra that "cleaner is better" and applied it as a logical progression of the work of those who came before him.

In fact the biggest change to the cover since the millennium is not related to design but rather to how many different covers are appropriate any given week. NFL and college football previews, for example, now run as many as seven regional covers each. SI readers have welcomed these additional covers as long as they remain in the tradition of the narrative poster that has set SI apart from the beginning.

What has never changed is a cover philosophy based on letting the photograph speak for itself. That is a fundamental thread in the original DNA of the franchise that still informs and energizes the look today.

TERRY McDONELL *came to SI in 2002 and is now the editor of the Sports Illustrated Group, which includes SI, SI.com and SI Golf.*

2000–2010

PETER WARRICK
January 10, 2000

SHAQUILLE O'NEAL
January 17, 2000

ISAAC BRUCE
January 24, 2000

JEVON KEARSE
January 31, 2000

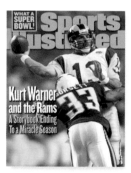
KURT WARNER
February 7, 2000

MICHAEL JORDAN
February 14, 2000

KEN GRIFFEY JR.
February 21, 2000

DANIELA PESTOVA
February 25, 2000

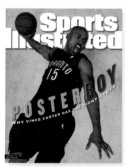
VINCE CARTER
February 28, 2000

NL CENTRAL POWER
March 6, 2000

FRANK THOMAS
March 13, 2000

MARCUS FIZER
March 20, 2000

PEDRO MARTINEZ
March 27, 2000

TIGER WOODS
April 3, 2000

MATEEN CLEAVES
April 10, 2000

THE WOEFUL CLIPPERS
April 17, 2000

KEYSHAWN JOHNSON
April 24, 2000

VLADIMIR GUERRERO
May 1, 2000

RANDY JOHNSON
May 8, 2000

HIGH TICKET PRICES
May 15, 2000

> " WHEN I WAS ON *the cover the first time my senior year at Penn State, my first reaction was shock. Since I was old enough to read the words 'sports' and 'illustrated,' it was something that I dreamed about.* "
>
> —Joe Jurevicius, *2003*

BOB KNIGHT
May 22, 2000

GRANT & BRYANT
May 29, 2000

ANNA KOURNIKOVA
June 5, 2000

KOBE BRYANT
June 12, 2000

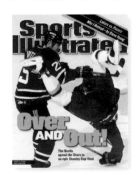

JASON ARNOTT
June 19, 2000

TIGER WOODS
June 26, 2000

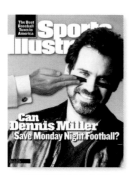

DENNIS MILLER
July 3, 2000

DAVID WELLS
July 10, 2000

JASON GIAMBI
July 17, 2000

LANCE ARMSTRONG
July 24, 2000

WILLIAM PERRY
July 31, 2000

MICHAEL VICK
August 14, 2000

MIKE PIAZZA
August 21, 2000

TIGER WOODS
August 28, 2000

RYAN LEAF
September 4, 2000

IVAN IVANKOV
September 11, 2000

BOB KNIGHT
September 18, 2000

MEGAN QUANN
September 25, 2000

MARION JONES
October 2, 2000

KURT WARNER
October 9, 2000

JIM EDMONDS
October 16, 2000

RICH GANNON
October 23, 2000

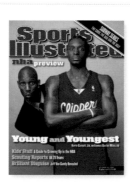

GARNETT & MILES
October 30, 2000

QUENTIN GRIFFIN
November 6, 2000

EDDIE GEORGE
November 13, 2000

SHANE BATTIER
November 20, 2000

TRAVIS MINOR
November 27, 2000

DAUNTE CULPEPPER
December 4, 2000

LAMAR SMITH
December 11, 2000

TIGER WOODS
December 18, 2000

CHRIS ROCK
December 25, 2000

QUENTIN GRIFFIN
January 8, 2001

RAVENS DEFENSE
January 15, 2001

AMANI TOOMER
January 22, 2001

SIRAGUSA & STRAHAN
January 29, 2001

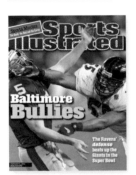

RAVENS WIN TITLE
February 5, 2001

THE XFL
February 12, 2001

SACRAMENTO KINGS
February 19, 2001

ELSA BENITEZ
February 23, 2001

DALE EARNHARDT
February 26, 2001

NOMAR GARCIAPARRA
March 5, 2001

MARIO LEMIEUX
March 12, 2001

NCAA PREVIEW
March 19, 2001

DEREK JETER
March 26, 2001

FINAL FOUR PREVIEW
April 2, 2001

DUNLEAVY & BATTIER
April 9, 2001

TIGER WOODS
April 16, 2001

ALLEN IVERSON
April 23, 2001

MATT LAWTON
April 30, 2001

JOHNNY UNITAS
May 7, 2001

IVERSON & CARTER
May 14, 2001

BARON DAVIS
May 21, 2001

ICHIRO SUZUKI
May 28, 2001

SHAQUILLE O'NEAL
June 4, 2001

LARRY WALKER
June 11, 2001

RAY BOURQUE
June 18, 2001

SHAQ & KOBE
June 25, 2001

DALLAS CHEERLEADERS
July 2, 2001

BRET BOONE
July 16, 2001

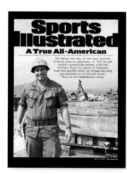

BOB KALSU
July 23, 2001

DAVID DUVAL
July 30, 2001

LANCE ARMSTRONG
August 6, 2001

OREGON FOOTBALL
August 13, 2001

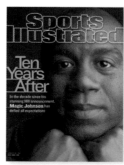

MAGIC JOHNSON
August 20, 2001

OVER- & UNDERRATED
August 27, 2001

MARSHALL FAULK
September 3, 2001

ROGER CLEMENS
September 10, 2001

DAVID CARR
September 17, 2001

SPORTS AFTER 9/11
September 24, 2001

JAY FIEDLER
October 1, 2001

BARRY BONDS
October 8, 2001

SIMMS & WILKERSON
October 15, 2001

DEREK JETER
October 22, 2001

MICHAEL JORDAN
October 29, 2001

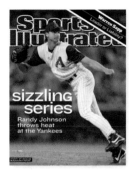

RANDY JOHNSON
November 5, 2001

ARIZONA WINS SERIES
November 12, 2001

JASON WILLIAMS
November 19, 2001

ERIC CROUCH
November 26, 2001

STEPHEN DAVIS
December 3, 2001

KORDELL STEWART
December 10, 2001

SCHILLING & JOHNSON
December 17, 2001

N.Y.C. FIREFIGHTERS
December 24, 2001

CLINTON PORTIS
January 7, 2002

MICHAEL JORDAN
January 14, 2002

SI'S COVER JINX
January 21, 2002

JASON KIDD
January 28, 2002

YAMILA DIAZ-RAHI
February 1, 2002

APOLO OHNO
February 4, 2002

McGINEST & WARNER
February 11, 2002

LeBRON JAMES
February 18, 2002

CHRIS WITTY
February 25, 2002

SARAH HUGHES
March 4, 2002

CHARLES BARKLEY
March 11, 2002

NICK COLLISON
March 18, 2002

JASON GIAMBI
March 25, 2002

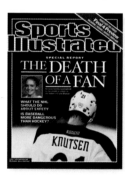

HOCKEY FAN KILLED
April 1, 2002

JUAN DIXON
April 8, 2002

TOM BRADY
April 15, 2002

TIGER WOODS
April 22, 2002

KENYON MARTIN
April 29, 2002

DIRK NOWITZKI
May 6, 2002

TREVOR HOFFMAN
May 13, 2002

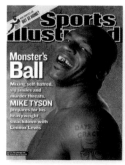

MIKE TYSON
May 20, 2002

CLINT MATHIS
May 27, 2002

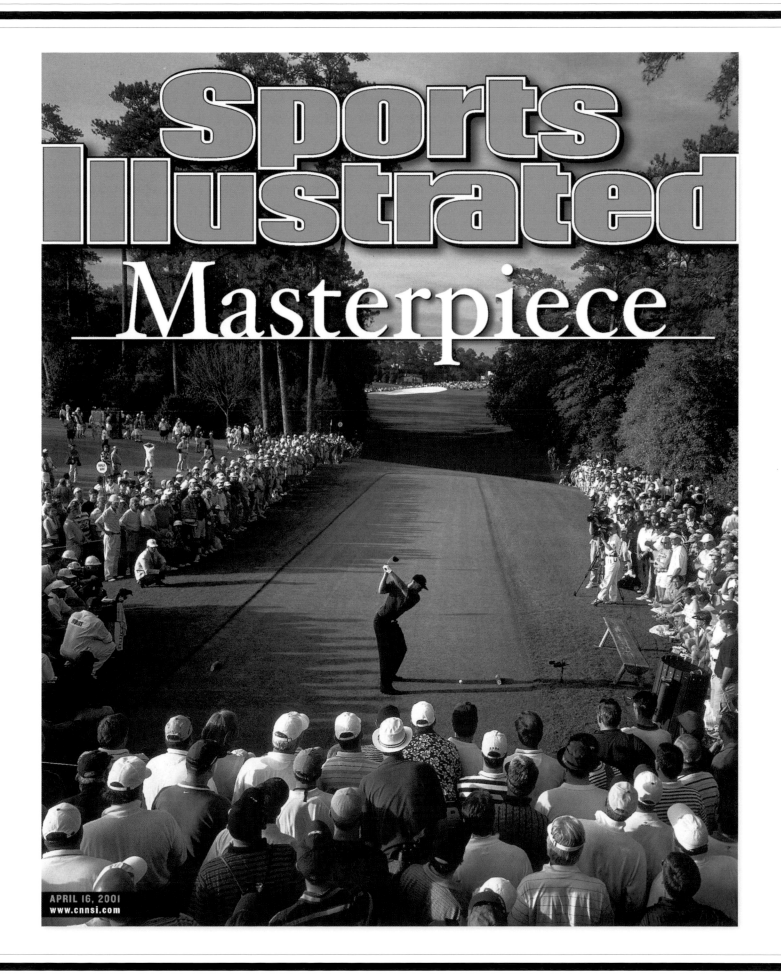

Sports Illustrated

Masterpiece

APRIL 16, 2001
www.cnnsi.com

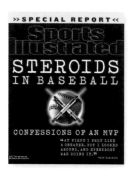

STEROIDS IN BASEBALL
June 3, 2002

KIDD & KOBE
June 10, 2002

SHAQUILLE O'NEAL
June 17, 2002

LANDON DONOVAN
June 24, 2002

DALE EARNHARDT JR.
July 1, 2002

ICHIRO SUZUKI
July 8, 2002

TED WILLIAMS
July 15, 2002

JOHN MADDEN
July 29, 2002

LANCE ARMSTRONG
August 5, 2002

TOMMIE HARRIS
August 12, 2002

DAVID CARR
August 19, 2002

ALFONSO SORIANO
August 26, 2002

RANDY MOSS
September 2, 2002

GRUDEN & SAPP
September 9, 2002

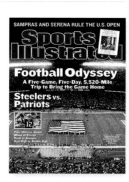

9/11—ONE YEAR LATER
September 16, 2002

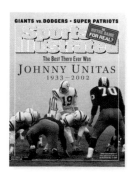

JOHNNY UNITAS
September 23, 2002

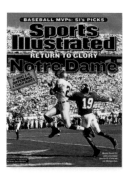

MAURICE STOVALL
September 30, 2002

BEST SPORTS COLLEGES
October 7, 2002

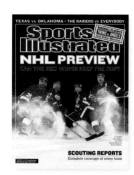

DETROIT RED WINGS
October 14, 2002

TRENT SMITH
October 21, 2002

YAO MING
October 28, 2002

ANGELS WIN SERIES
November 4, 2002

JOEY HARRINGTON
November 11, 2002

BRIAN BROHM
November 18, 2002

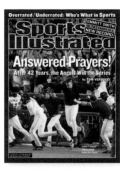

GARDNER & WALTON
November 25, 2002

MAURICE CLARETT
December 2, 2002

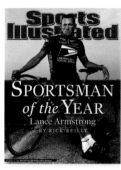

RICKY WILLIAMS
December 9, 2002

LANCE ARMSTRONG
December 16, 2002

BRETT FAVRE
December 23, 2002

YEAR IN REVIEW
December 30, 2002

CRAIG KRENZEL
January 13, 2003

RICH GANNON
January 20, 2003

SAPP & GANNON
January 27, 2003

JOE JUREVICIUS
February 3, 2003

YAO MING
February 10, 2003

MICHAEL JORDAN
February 17, 2003

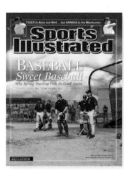

SPRING TRAINING
February 24, 2003

PETRA NEMCOVA
February 25, 2003

KOBE BRYANT
March 3, 2003

185

CLIFF HAWKINS
March 10, 2003

KIRBY PUCKETT
March 17, 2003

MARCH MADNESS
March 24, 2003

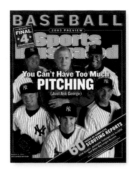

YANKEES PITCHING
March 31, 2003

FINAL FOUR PREVIEW
April 7, 2003

CARMELO ANTHONY
April 14, 2003

MIKE WEIR
April 21, 2003

CARSON PALMER
April 28, 2003

MINORITY INFLUENCE
May 5, 2003

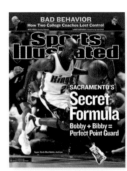

BOBBY JACKSON
May 12, 2003

JASON KIDD
May 19, 2003

SERENA WILLIAMS
May 26, 2003

ROGER CLEMENS
June 2, 2003

TIM DUNCAN
June 9, 2003

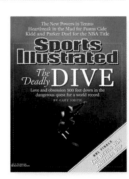

DEEP DIVERS
June 16, 2003

DAVID ROBINSON
June 23, 2003

BO JACKSON
June 30, 2003

WOOD & PRIOR
July 7, 2003

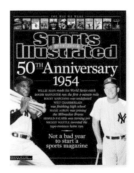

MAYS & MANTLE
July 14, 2003

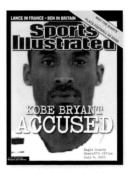

KOBE BRYANT
July 28, 2003

LANCE ARMSTRONG
August 4, 2003

CRAIG KRENZEL
August 11, 2003

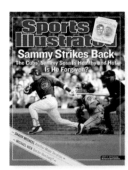

BILL PARCELLS
August 18, 2003

SAMMY SOSA
August 25, 2003

KURT WARNER
September 1, 2003

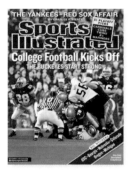

OHIO STATE FOOTBALL
September 8, 2003

SAM ADAMS
September 15, 2003

MIA HAMM
September 22, 2003

JASON FIFE
September 29, 2003

JAKE PLUMMER
October 6, 2003

PEDRO MARTINEZ
October 13, 2003

JASON WHITE
October 20, 2003

LeBRON JAMES
October 27, 2003

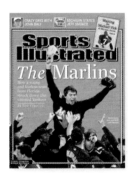

JOSH BECKETT
November 3, 2003

SI COVERS
November 10, 2003

TRENT GREEN
November 17, 2003

TAURASI & OKAFOR
November 24, 2003

CHRIS PERRY
December 1, 2003

KYLE TURLEY
December 8, 2003

DUNCAN & ROBINSON
December 15, 2003

187

PEYTON MANNING
December 22, 2003

CARMELO ANTHONY
December 29, 2003

PETE ROSE
January 12, 2004

DONOVAN McNABB
January 19, 2004

MUHSIN MUHAMMAD
January 26, 2004

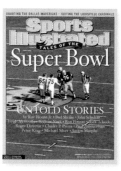

SUPER BOWL TALES
February 2, 2004

TOM BRADY
February 9, 2004

VERONICA VAREKOVA
February 10, 2004

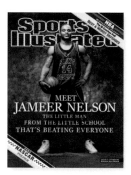

JAMEER NELSON
February 16, 2004

ALEX RODRIGUEZ
February 23, 2004

MINNESOTA T-WOLVES
March 1, 2004

SEBASTIAN TELFAIR
March 8, 2004

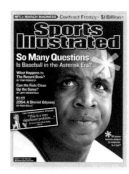

BARRY BONDS
March 15, 2004

MARCH MADNESS
March 22, 2004

CHUCK DAVIS
March 29, 2004

KERRY WOOD
April 5, 2004

EMEKA OKAFOR
April 12, 2004

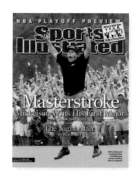

PHIL MICKELSON
April 19, 2004

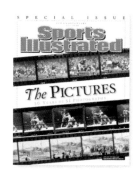

SI PHOTOGRAPHY
April 26, 2004

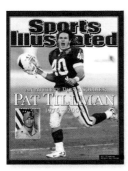

PAT TILLMAN
May 3, 2004

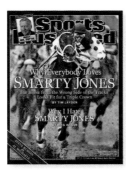

SMARTY JONES
May 10, 2004

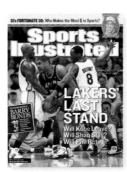

LAKERS VS. SPURS
May 17, 2004

ROGER CLEMENS
May 24, 2004

KEVIN GARNETT
May 31, 2004

DEREK JETER
June 7, 2004

KEN GRIFFEY JR.
June 14, 2004

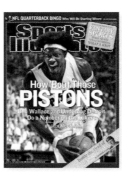

BEN WALLACE
June 21, 2004

LANCE ARMSTRONG
June 28, 2004

MANNY RAMIREZ
July 5, 2004

MARIA SHARAPOVA
July 12, 2004

KOBE & SHAQ
July 26, 2004

MICHAEL PHELPS
August 2, 2004

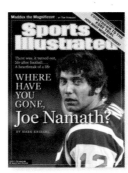

JOE NAMATH
August 9, 2004

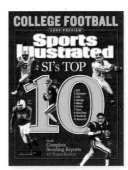

COLLEGE FOOTBALL
August 16, 2004

MICHAEL PHELPS
August 23, 2004

U.S. SOFTBALL TEAM
August 30, 2004

TOM BRADY
September 6, 2004

CURT SCHILLING
September 13, 2004

MICHAEL VICK
September 20, 2004

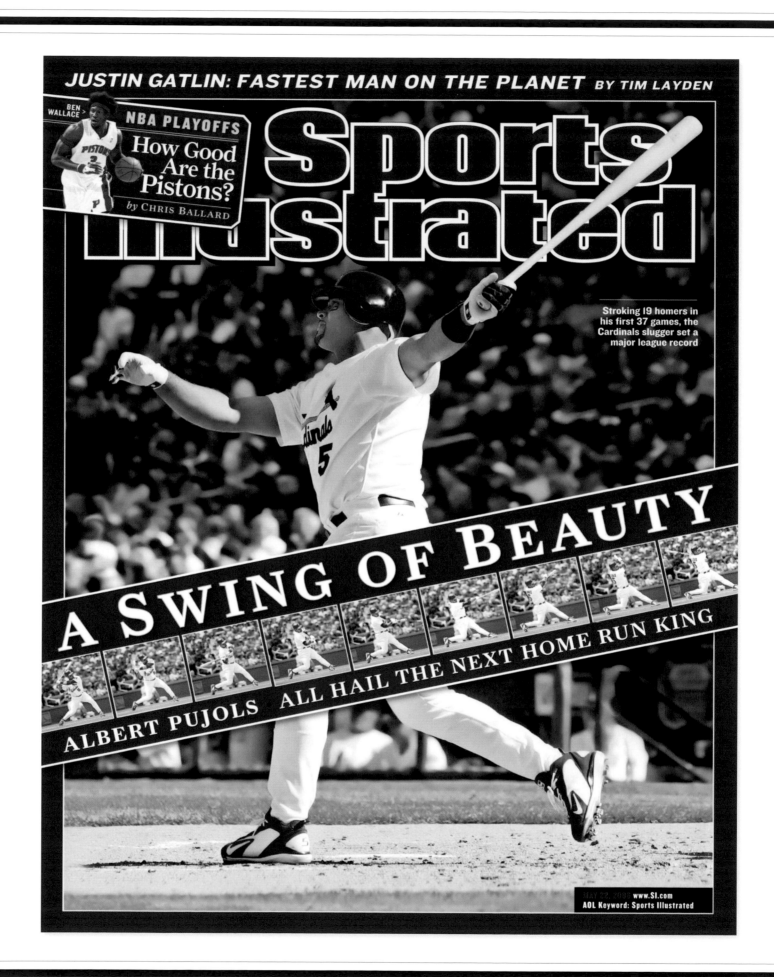

JUSTIN GATLIN: FASTEST MAN ON THE PLANET BY TIM LAYDEN

BEN WALLACE

NBA PLAYOFFS
How Good Are the Pistons?
by CHRIS BALLARD

Sports Illustrated

Stroking 19 homers in his first 37 games, the Cardinals slugger set a major league record

A SWING OF BEAUTY

ALBERT PUJOLS   ALL HAIL THE NEXT HOME RUN KING

MAY 22, 2006 www.SI.com
AOL Keyword: Sports Illustrated

50TH ANNIVERSARY
September 27, 2004

ALBERT PUJOLS
October 4, 2004

ADRIAN PETERSON
October 11, 2004

TOM BRADY
October 18, 2004

SHAQUILLE O'NEAL
October 25, 2004

WORLD SERIES
November 1, 2004

RED SOX WIN SERIES
November 8, 2004

WARD & BURRESS
November 15, 2004

RASHAD McCANTS
November 22, 2004

RON ARTEST
November 29, 2004

BOSTON RED SOX
December 6, 2004

REGGIE BUSH
December 13, 2004

PEYTON MANNING
December 20, 2004

SHAQUILLE O'NEAL
December 27, 2004

05

MATT LEINART
January 10, 2005

REGGIE WAYNE
January 17, 2005

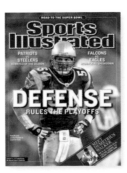

TEDY BRUSCHI
January 24, 2005

JEREMIAH TROTTER
January 31, 2005

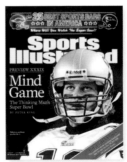

TOM BRADY
February 7, 2005

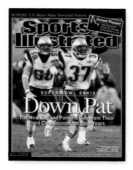

PATRIOTS WIN TITLE
February 14, 2005

CAROLYN MURPHY
February 18, 2005

LeBRON JAMES
February 21, 2005

DAYTONA 500
February 28, 2005

DEE BROWN
March 7, 2005

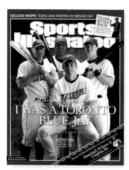

VERDUCCI & THE JAYS
March 14, 2005

MARCH MADNESS
March 21, 2005

STEROIDS IN BASEBALL
March 28, 2005

JETER & DAMON
April 4, 2005

SEAN MAY
April 11, 2005

TIGER WOODS
April 18, 2005

STOUDEMIRE & O'NEAL
April 25, 2005

NFL DRAFT
May 2, 2005

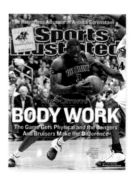

BEN WALLACE
May 9, 2005

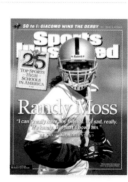

RANDY MOSS
May 16, 2005

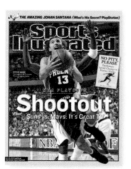

STEVE NASH
May 23, 2005

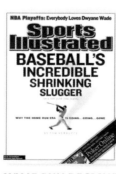

HOME RUN DECLINE
May 30, 2005

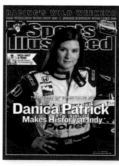

DANICA PATRICK
June 6, 2005

STREET BALL
June 13, 2005

LANCE ARMSTRONG
June 20, 2005

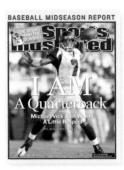

WALLACE & DUNCAN
June 27, 2005

MICHAEL VICK
July 4, 2005

JENNIE FINCH
July 11, 2005

TIGER WOODS
July 25, 2005

LANCE ARMSTRONG
August 1, 2005

AHMAN GREEN
August 8, 2005

REGGIE BUSH
August 15, 2005

PHIL MICKELSON
August 22, 2005

JEFF FRANCOEUR
August 29, 2005

JAKE DELHOMME
September 5, 2005

TED GINN JR.
September 12, 2005

LOUISIANA FOOTBALL
September 19, 2005

McNABB & OWENS
September 26, 2005

PLAYOFF PREVIEW
October 3, 2005

BRODIE CROYLE
October 10, 2005

DWIGHT FREENEY
October 17, 2005

ARTEST & BIRD
October 24, 2005

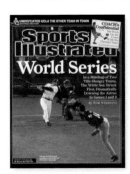

WHITE SOX VS. ASTROS
October 31, 2005

MANNING VS. BRADY
November 7, 2005

TROY POLAMALU
November 14, 2005

COLLEGE BASKETBALL
November 21, 2005

JOE PATERNO
November 28, 2005

VINCE YOUNG
December 5, 2005

TOM BRADY
December 12, 2005

SHAUN ALEXANDER
December 19, 2005

BUSH & LEINART
December 26, 2005

VINCE YOUNG
January 9, 2006

JEROME BETTIS
January 16, 2006

BEN ROETHLISBERGER
January 23, 2006

JEROME BETTIS
January 30, 2006

U.S. SKI TEAM
February 6, 2006

HINES WARD
February 13, 2006

SWIMSUIT ALL-STARS
February 17, 2006

SHAUN WHITE
February 20, 2006

U.S. SNOWBOARDERS
February 27, 2006

MORRISON & REDICK
March 6, 2006

BARRY BONDS
March 13, 2006

MARCH MADNESS
March 20, 2006

LAMAR BUTLER
March 27, 2006

ALBERT PUJOLS
April 3, 2006

JOAKIM NOAH
April 10, 2006

PHIL MICKELSON
April 17, 2006

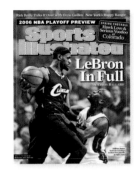

LeBRON JAMES
April 24, 2006

VINCE YOUNG
May 1, 2006

LANCE ARMSTRONG
May 8, 2006

BARRY BONDS
May 15, 2006

ALBERT PUJOLS
May 22, 2006

CARSON PALMER
May 29, 2006

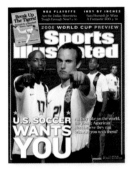

U.S. SOCCER TEAM
June 5, 2006

DWYANE WADE
June 12, 2006

DAVID ORTIZ
June 19, 2006

PHIL MICKELSON
June 26, 2006

LAWRENCE TAYLOR
July 3, 2006

NEW YORK METS
July 17, 2006

REGGIE BUSH
July 24, 2006

TIGER WOODS
July 31, 2006

JOE MAUER
August 7, 2006

NFL TRAINING CAMPS
August 14, 2006

OHIO STATE FOOTBALL
August 21, 2006

JUSTIN VERLANDER
August 28, 2006

JOEY PORTER
September 4, 2006

PAT TILLMAN
September 11, 2006

OHIO STATE FOOTBALL
September 18, 2006

ALEX RODRIGUEZ
September 25, 2006

STEELERS VS. BENGALS
October 2, 2006

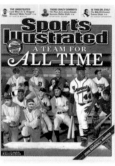

SI'S ALLTIME TEAM
October 9, 2006

SEC FOOTBALL
October 16, 2006

LeBRON JAMES
October 23, 2006

CHAD JOHNSON
October 30, 2006

DAVID ECKSTEIN
November 6, 2006

RAY LEWIS
November 13, 2006

HIBBERT & WALLACE
November 20, 2006

TROY SMITH
November 27, 2006

BRETT FAVRE
December 4, 2006

DWYANE WADE
December 11, 2006

FACES IN THE CROWD
December 15, 2006

VINCE YOUNG
December 18, 2006

LADANIAN TOMLINSON
December 25, 2006

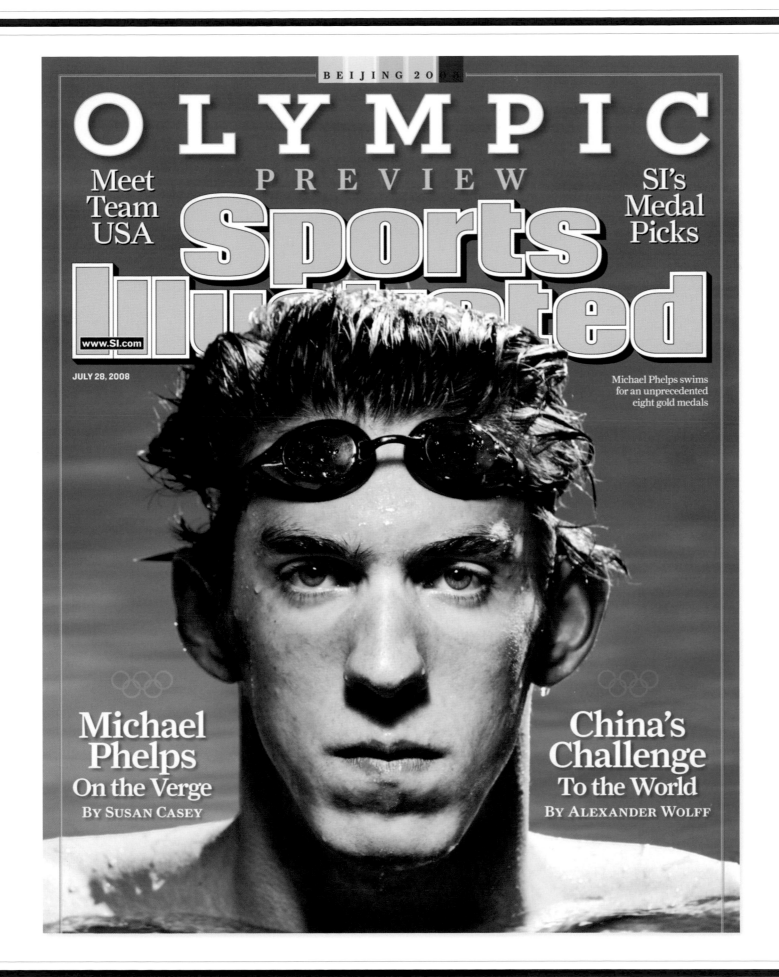

BEIJING 2008

OLYMPIC

PREVIEW

Meet
Team
USA

SI's
Medal
Picks

Sports Illustrated

www.SI.com

JULY 28, 2008

Michael Phelps swims
for an unprecedented
eight gold medals

Michael Phelps
On the Verge
BY SUSAN CASEY

China's Challenge
To the World
BY ALEXANDER WOLFF

JEFF GARCIA
January 8, 2007

CHRIS LEAK
January 15, 2007

DREW BREES
January 22, 2007

PEYTON MANNING
January 29, 2007

BRIAN URLACHER
February 5, 2007

PEYTON MANNING
February 12, 2007

BEYONCÉ
February 15, 2007

KEVIN DURANT
February 19, 2007

PINIELLA & SORIANO
February 26, 2007

OHIO STATE SPORTS
March 5, 2007

SPORTS & CLIMATE CHANGE
March 12, 2007

MARCH MADNESS
March 19, 2007

DAISUKE MATSUZAKA
March 26, 2007

TIGER WOODS
April 2, 2007

COREY BREWER
April 9, 2007

TIGER WOODS
April 16, 2007

NASH & NOWITZKI
April 23, 2007

ADRIAN PETERSON
April 30, 2007

DE LA HOYA VS. MAYWEATHER
May 7, 2007

GRADY SIZEMORE
May 14, 2007

BARRY BONDS
May 21, 2007

ULTIMATE FIGHTING
May 28, 2007

TIM DUNCAN
June 4, 2007

LeBRON JAMES
June 11, 2007

NEW YORK METS
June 18, 2007

SAN ANTONIO SPURS
June 25, 2007

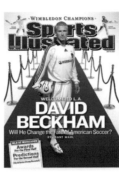

HANSON BROTHERS
July 2, 2007

DAVID BECKHAM
July 16, 2007

HANK AARON
July 23, 2007

THE NFL'S BIG HITS
July 30, 2007

JAMAL LEWIS
August 6, 2007

BARRY BONDS
August 13, 2007

MIKE HART
August 20, 2007

NICK SABAN
August 27, 2007

PEYTON MANNING
September 3, 2007

DEXTER JACKSON
September 10, 2007

RANDY MOSS
September 17, 2007

USC FOOTBALL
September 24, 2007

JONATHAN PAPELBON
October 1, 2007

JIMMY ROLLINS
October 8, 2007

JEFF FRANCIS
October 15, 2007

TOM BRADY
October 22, 2007

BOSTON CELTICS
October 29, 2007

JONATHAN PAPELBON
November 5, 2007

PATRIOTS DEFENSE
November 12, 2007

WHITE & PRUITT
November 19, 2007

KERRY MEIER
November 26, 2007

CHASE DANIEL
December 3, 2007

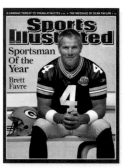

BRETT FAVRE
December 10, 2007

KEVIN EVERETT
December 17, 2007

YEAR IN PICTURES
December 24, 2007

BILL BELICHICK
December 31, 2007

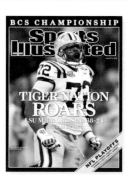

GLENN DORSEY
January 14, 2008

BRETT FAVRE
January 21, 2008

ELI MANNING
January 28, 2008

SUPER BOWL PREVIEW
February 4, 2008

DAVID TYREE
February 11, 2008

MARISA MILLER
February 15, 2008

DALE EARNHARDT JR.
February 18, 2008

JOHAN SANTANA
February 25, 2008

JASON KIDD
March 3, 2008

TYLER HANSBROUGH
March 10, 2008

BRETT FAVRE
March 17, 2008

BRANDON RUSH
March 24, 2008

BASEBALL PREVIEW
March 31, 2008

TYLER HANSBROUGH
April 7, 2008

MARIO CHALMERS
April 14, 2008

BRYANT & GARNETT
April 21, 2008

JOHNNY UNITAS
April 28, 2008

KOSUKE FUKUDOME
May 5, 2008

CHRIS PAUL
May 12, 2008

DANICA PATRICK
May 19, 2008

BIZARRO BASEBALL
May 26, 2008

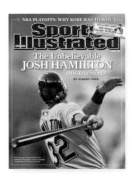

JOSH HAMILTON
June 2, 2008

LAKERS VS. CELTICS
June 9, 2008

BRYANT & PIERCE
June 16, 2008

TIGER WOODS
June 23, 2008

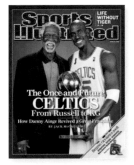

RUSSELL & GARNETT
June 30, 2008

TIM LINCECUM
July 7, 2008

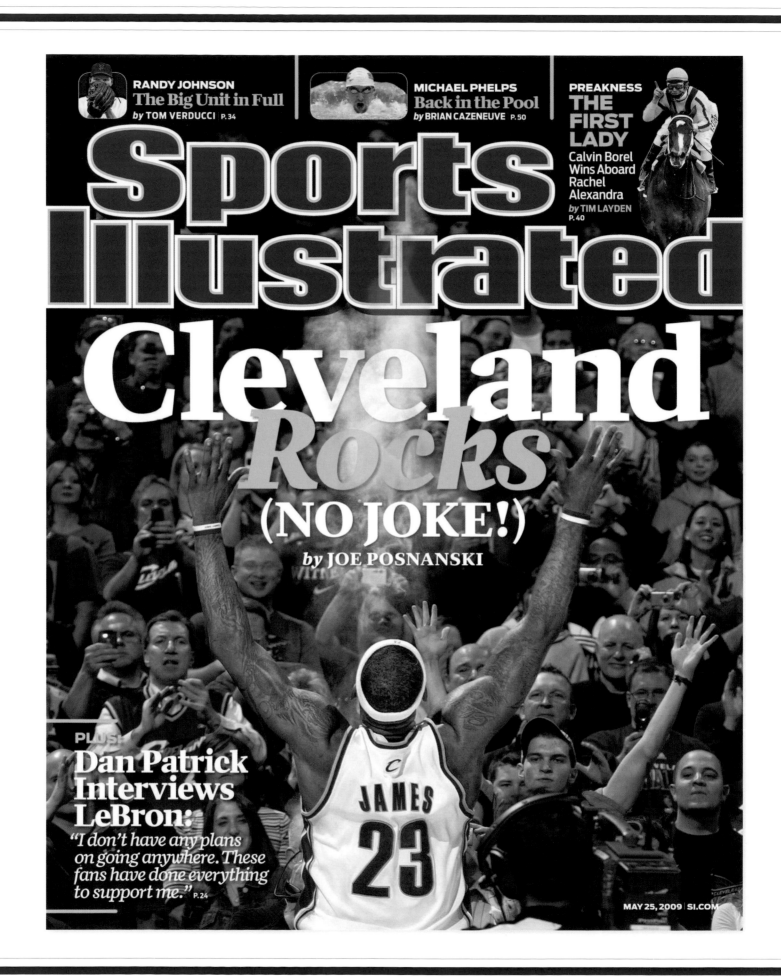

RANDY JOHNSON
The Big Unit in Full
by TOM VERDUCCI P.34

MICHAEL PHELPS
Back in the Pool
by BRIAN CAZENEUVE P.50

PREAKNESS
THE FIRST LADY
Calvin Borel Wins Aboard Rachel Alexandra
by TIM LAYDEN
P. 40

Sports Illustrated

Cleveland
Rocks
(NO JOKE!)
by JOE POSNANSKI

PLUS
Dan Patrick Interviews LeBron:
"I don't have any plans on going anywhere. These fans have done everything to support me." P.24

MAY 25, 2009 | SI.COM

FEDERER & NADAL
July 14, 2008

MICHAEL PHELPS
July 28, 2008

DAVID TYREE
August 4, 2008

COLLEGE FOOTBALL
August 11, 2008

MICHAEL PHELPS
August 18, 2008

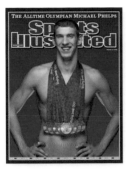

MICHAEL PHELPS
August 25, 2008

DONOVAN McNABB
September 1, 2008

GLEN COFFEE
September 8, 2008

BRETT FAVRE
September 15, 2008

YANKEE STADIUM
September 22, 2008

ARAMIS RAMIREZ
September 29, 2008

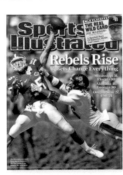

GREG HARDY
October 6, 2008

MANNY RAMIREZ
October 13, 2008

COLT McCOY
October 20, 2008

ELTON BRAND
October 27, 2008

PHILLIES VS. RAYS
November 3, 2008

ALBERT HAYNESWORTH
November 10, 2008

COLLEGE BASKETBALL
November 17, 2008

JIMMIE JOHNSON
November 24, 2008

SAM BRADFORD
December 1, 2008

203

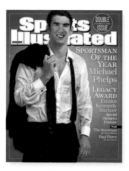

MICHAEL PHELPS
December 8, 2008

YEAR IN PICTURES
December 12, 2008

TIM TEBOW
December 15, 2008

LAMARR WOODLEY
December 22, 2008

MICHAEL VICK'S DOGS
December 29, 2008

DeSEAN JACKSON
January 12, 2009

WASHINGTON & HOLMES
January 19, 2009

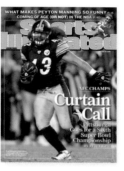

TROY POLAMALU
January 26, 2009

LeBRON JAMES
February 2, 2009

SANTONIO HOLMES
February 9, 2009

BAR REFAELI
February 13, 2009

ALEX RODRIGUEZ
February 16, 2009

COLE HAMELS
February 23, 2009

TIGER WOODS
March 2, 2009

MARCH MAYHEM
March 9, 2009

ALBERT PUJOLS
March 16, 2009

MARCH MADNESS
March 23, 2009

LEVANCE FIELDS
March 30, 2009

CC SABATHIA
April 6, 2009

TYLER HANSBROUGH
April 13, 2009

DWIGHT HOWARD
April 20, 2009

NFL DRAFT PREVIEW
April 27, 2009

ZACK GREINKE
May 4, 2009

MINE THAT BIRD
May 11, 2009

MANNY RAMIREZ
May 18, 2009

LeBRON JAMES
May 25, 2009

TOM BRADY
June 1, 2009

BRYCE HARPER
June 8, 2009

ROGER FEDERER
June 15, 2009

KOBE BRYANT
June 22, 2009

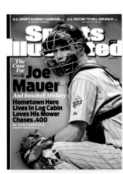

JOE MAUER
June 29, 2009

ED THOMAS
July 6, 2009

RYAN & SEAVER
July 13, 2009

TIM TEBOW
July 27, 2009

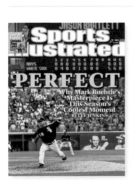

MARK BUEHRLE
August 3, 2009

JASON CAMPBELL
August 10, 2009

COLLEGE FOOTBALL
August 17, 2009

MARC BUONICONTI
August 24, 2009

USAIN BOLT
August 31, 2009

BEN ROETHLISBERGER
September 7, 2009

DEZ BRYANT
September 14, 2009

ADRIAN PETERSON
September 21, 2009

DETROIT TIGERS
September 28, 2009

MARIANO RIVERA
October 5, 2009

DANIEL GRAHAM
October 12, 2009

TIM TEBOW
October 19, 2009

O'NEAL & JAMES
October 26, 2009

RYAN HOWARD
November 2, 2009

DEREK JETER
November 9, 2009

PEYTON MANNING
November 16, 2009

SHERRON COLLINS
November 23, 2009

MARK INGRAM
November 30, 2009

DEREK JETER
December 7, 2009

YEAR IN PICTURES
December 11, 2009

COLIN PEEK
December 14, 2009

STEPHEN COLBERT
December 21, 2009

LeBRON JAMES
December 28, 2009

MILES AUSTIN
January 11, 2010

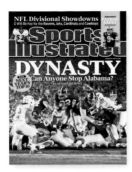

MARK INGRAM
January 18, 2010

BRETT FAVRE
January 25, 2010

DREW BREES
February 1, 2010

LINDSEY VONN
February 8, 2010

BROOKLYN DECKER
February 12, 2010

DREW BREES
February 15, 2010

APOLO OHNO
February 22, 2010

U.S. SKIERS
March 1, 2010

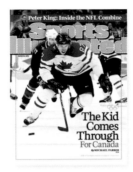

SIDNEY CROSBY
March 8, 2010

OLYMPIC PICTURES
March 10, 2010

MATT WIETERS
March 15, 2010

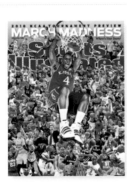

MARCH MADNESS
March 22, 2010

ALI FAROKHMANESH
March 29, 2010

ROY HALLADAY
April 5, 2010

JON SCHEYER
April 12, 2010

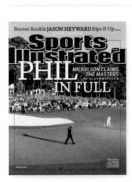

PHIL MICKELSON
April 19, 2010

SAM BRADFORD
April 26, 2010

YANKEES QUARTET
May 3, 2010

BEN ROETHLISBERGER
May 10, 2010

SHAQUILLE O'NEAL
May 17, 2010

Acknowledgments

SPECIAL THANKS GO OUT TO Steve Fine, Karen Carpenter, Geoff Michaud, Dan Larkin, Bob Thompson and the Sports Illustrated Imaging Group, Don Delliquanti, Joy Birdsong, Georgia Hoffman, Suzanne Noli, Leon Avelino, Andy Borinstein, John Reese and Liz Greco. An extra special note of gratitude goes to all those cover subjects who graciously posed through the years and agreed to smile—or maybe even snarl menacingly—just one more time for the cameras.

Looking Back *Muhammad Ali was photographed for SI's 35th anniversary cover in 1989 holding the first issue on which he appeared, in 1963.*

TIME HOME ENTERTAINMENT: Richard Fraiman, PUBLISHER; Steven Sandonato, GENERAL MANAGER; Carol Pittard, EXECUTIVE DIRECTOR, MARKETING SERVICES; Tom Mifsud, DIRECTOR, RETAIL & SPECIAL SALES; Peter Harper, DIRECTOR, NEW PRODUCT DEVELOPMENT; Laura Adam, DIRECTOR, BOOKAZINE DEVELOPMENT & MARKETING; Joy Butts, PUBLISHING DIRECTOR, BRAND MARKETING; Helen Wan, ASSISTANT GENERAL COUNSEL; Anne-Michelle Gallero, DESIGN & PREPRESS MANAGER; Susan Chodakiewicz, BOOK PRODUCTION MANAGER; Allison Parker, ASSOCIATE BRAND MANAGER; Alex Voznesenskiy, ASSOCIATE PREPRESS MANAGER

COVERS CREDITS

Walter Iooss Jr. (239), Neil Leifer (164), Heinz Kluetmeier (125), John Biever (124), Manny Millan (116), Peter Read Miller (105), John G. Zimmerman (102), John Iacono (83), James Drake (79), John W. McDonough (64), Ronald C. Modra (60), Al Tielemans (58), Tony Triolo (49), Jerry Cooke (44), Richard Meek (44), Hy Peskin (42), Sheedy & Long (39), Andy Hayt (38), Mark Kauffman (37), Richard Mackson (36), Bob Rosato (35), Getty Images (34), V.J. Lovero (33), Robert Beck (32), Rich Clarkson (32), Chuck Solomon (32), Damian Strohmeyer (32), Simon Bruty (30), Jerry Wachter (29), David E. Klutho (28), Lane Stewart (28), Michael O'Neill (24), Bill Frakes (23), Marvin E. Newman (21), Fred Kaplan (18), Brian Lanker (15), Jay Maisel (15), Eric Schweikardt (14), Donald Moss (13), Tony Tomsic (13), Robert Huntzinger (12), Herb Scharfman (12), Toni Frissell (11), Frank Mullins (11), Bernard Fuchs (10), Francis Golden (10), LIFE (10), NBA Photos (10), Bill Smith (10), AP (9), Gregory Heisler (9), Michael J. Lebrecht II (9), Dick Raphael (9), Robert Riger (9), Daniel Schwartz (9), Arthur Shay (9), David Walberg (9), Neal Barr (8), Phil Bath (8), David Bergman (8), Corbis (8), Robert Handville (8), Greg Nelson (8), Paul Bereswill (7), David Goodnow (7), Phillip Leonian (7), Fred Lyon (7), Brad Mangin (7), Ken Regan/Camera 5 (7), George Tiedemann (7), Theo Westenberger (7), Jacqueline Duvoisin (6), Joern Gerdts (6), Peter Gregoire (6), Ernst Haas (6), John D. Hanlon (6), Richard Jeffery (6), Arnold Newman (6), Steve Powell (6), Jeffery A. Salter (6), Brian Seed (6), Bill Eppridge (5), Will Hart (5), Lynn Johnson (5), Caryn Levy (5), Matt Mahurin (5), Robert Peak (5), Mickey Pfleger (5), Gerard Rancinan (5), Anthony Ravielli (7), Reuters (5), Carl Skalak (5), Focus on Sports (5), Andrew D. Bernstein (4), Jon Brenneis (4), Darren Carroll (4), Stephen Green-Armytage (4), John Langley Howard (4), Carl Iwasaki (4), Paul Kennedy (4), Edward Kasper (4), Bob Martin (4), Joe McNally (4), Co Rentmeester (4), Manny Rubio (4), Howard Schatz (4), Sportschrome USA (4), Fred Vuich (4), Dan Weiner (4), Jeff Wong (4), Dan Baliotti (3), Gary Bogdon (3), Richard Corman (3), Gerry Cranham (3), Paolo Curto (3), Arthur Daley (3), Hank DeLespinasse (3), Tony Duffy (3), Jim Gund (3), Hans Knopf (3), George Lange (3), Raphael Mazzucco (3), Clay Patrick McBride (3), Craig Molenhouse (3), A.Y. Owen (3), Morton Roberts (3), Steve Schapiro (3), George Silk (3), Walt Spitzmiller (3), Robert Weaver (3), Garry Winogrand (3), Julian Allen (2), Thomas B. Allen (2), Harry Benson (2), Lou Capozzola (2), Christa (2), Contact Press Images (2), Louise Dahl-Wolfe (2), Roy DeCarava (2), Robert Erdmann (2), Greg Foster (2), Rich Frishman (2), Farrell Grehan (2), Bob Gomel (2), Helmut Gritscher (2), Amy Guip (2), Philippe Halsman (2), Phil Huber (2), Sandy Huffaker (2), Icon SMI (2), Art Kane (2), Jonas Karlsson (2), David Liam Kyle (2), Bob Landry (2), Russell Lee (2), Steve Lipofsky (2), Tom Lynn (2), Athos Menaboni (2), Jean Moss (2), Dickran Palulian (2), C.F. Payne (2), Art Rickerby (2), Bill Robbins (2), Raeanne Rubenstein (2), Eric Schaal (2), Lawrence Schiller (2), Mary Schilpp (2), Harvey Schmidt (2), Aaron Shikler (2), Bud Simpson (2), Brian Smith (2), Edward Sorel (2), Greg Spalenka (2), Ozzie Sweet (2), US Presswire (2), Burk Uzzle (2), Ed Vebell (2), Stephen Wilkes (2), Wireimage.com (2), Carl Yarbrough (2), Ylla (2), 2000 NHL Images, Mark Abrahams, Russ Adams, Agence Tempsport, Agence Vandystadt, Roy Anderson, Ron Angle, Davila Arellano, Ray Atkeson, Mark Bagley, Bill Ballenberg, Clyde Banks, Jeff Bark, Bruce Bennett, George Bennett, Walter Bennett, Claus Bergmann, Peter Biro, Barry Blackman, John Blaustein, Moshe Brakha, Austin Briggs, John Bryson, Dan Budnik, John Burgess, Philip Burke, Tom Burnside, Steve Cadrain, Cal Sport Media, E.J. Camp, Mary Beth Camp, Cornell Capa,

R.J. Capak, Gwendolen Cates, Fred E. Chez, Elgin Ciampi, Howell Conant, Pier Consagra, Lee Crum, Culver Pictures, The Daily Oklahoman, Dick Darcey, Hollinger Davos, Yves Debraine, Melchior DiGiacomo, Joe DiMaggio, Harvey Dinnerstein, Tom DiPace, Bob Donnan, Keith Dorris, Brian Drake, Anthony Edgeworth, Richard Erdoes, Elliott Erwitt, ESPN, ETSU, N.R. Farbman, Donna Ferrato, Sheldon Fink, Graham Finlayson, Ed Fisher, James F. Flores, Bart Forbes, Andre Francois, Mark Fredrickson, Lee Friedlander, Ormond Gigli, Guy Gillette, Milton Glaser, Frank Golden, Lynn Goldsmith, Steven Goldstein, Aaron Goodman, Allan Grant, Stephen Green, Lois Greenfield, Arthur Griffin, Robert Grossman, Curt Gunther, Robert Gwathmey, Richard Hagedohm, Robert Halmi, Mark Hanauer, Andrew Hancock, Jennifer S. Hayes, John Haynes, HBO, Shel Hershorn, Richard Hess, Marc Hispard, Russell Hoban, Norris Hoyt, John Huehnergrath, John Huet, Tom Hutchins, Indianapolis Police Dept., Bob Isear, Russell James, John F. Jaqua, Diane Johnson, Trevor Jones, George Kalinsky, Jan Kalsu-McLauchlin, John F. Kenney, Bob Kinmonth, Daniel Kirk, Wallace Kirkland, David Kitz, Jessica Kluetmeier, Henry Koehler, Todd Korol, Mike Kullen, Anita Kunz, David LaChapelle, Larry Spangler Productions, Lisa Larsen, George Leavens, Joe Lertola, Erich Lessing, Leviton/Atlanta, Scott Jordan Levy, Malcolm T. Liepke, George Long, Los Angeles Times, Jeffrey Lowe, Gene Lower, Dennis Luzak, Jerome Martin, Kim Massie, Sharon McCormack, Roy McKie, Bob Miller, Buck Miller, MLB Photos, George Moffett, David Moore, R.D. Moore, Del Mulkey, Bob Mummery, Patrick Murphy-Racey, Martin Nathan, National Baseball Library, Anthony Neste, New York Daily News, David Noyes, Michael O'Brien, Michael O'Bryon, David O'Keefe, Jeff Olson, John Olson, Don Ornitz, Herbert Orth, Dennis Ortiz-Lopez, Fred Otnes, Manuello Paganelli, Kourken Pakchanian, Gabe Palaccio, Glenn Palmer-Smith, Daniel Pelavin, Lynn Pelham, Irving Penn, PGA Tour, Coles Phinizy, Richard Pilling, Polaris, James Porto, Mike Powell, The Press Democrat, Princeton University, Louis Psihoyos, Thomas Rampy, Joe Raymond, Mike Reinhardt, Larry Rivers, Peter Robinson, Rocky Mountain News, D.P. Rodewald, Robert Rogers, Ben Rose, Morris Rosenfeld, Daniel Rubin, Marcia Rules, John Sadovy, Philip Saltonstall, Lewis B. Sanborn, R. Satakopan, Al Satterwhite, Chuck Schmidt, Bruce L. Schwartzman, Schwartzman Sports, Abe Seltzer, Sam Shaw, Joseph Sheppard, Stewart Shining, Burt Silverman, Robert Silvers, Marc Simont, Arthur Singer, SIPA/Special Features, Brett Smith, J. Frederick Smith, Bob Stanley, Star-News, Staten Island Advocate, Philip D. Stearns, Ed Stein, Ted Streshinsky, David Strick, John A. Sugar, Mark Summers, Surfer magazine, Swiss Himalaya Expedition, Syracuse University, Takeo Tanuma, TGPL, Steve Thompson, James Thurber, Tillman Family, TIME, Dan Todd, Transcendental Graphics, Transfilm Inc., Brad Trent, TSN/Icon SMI, Pete Turner, Tomi Ungerer, University of Miami, Lauren Uram, Nittin Vadakul, Antoine Verglas, Dr. Roman Vishniac, Stefan Warter, The Washington Post, The Waterloo Courier, Albert Watson, Cliff Watts, Frank White, Coby Whitmore, James Whitmore, Leigh Wiener, Larry Williams, Steven C. Wilson, Malcolm Wister, Thomas E. Witte, Henry Wolff, Willis A. Wood, Woodfin Camp, Works NY, Joe Zeff, David Drew Zingg, Zuma Press

ADDITIONAL CREDITS

Page 10: Jerry Cooke; Page 11: Jon Brenneis; Page 15: Matt Rourke/AFP/Getty Images (Carter), Rich Clarkson (Auerbach); Page 16: John G. Zimmerman (Hornung), Malcolm Emmons/US Presswire (Sims), Long Photography (Walton); Page 18: Al Tielemans (White), Robert Beck (Kwan), Simon Bruty (Smarty Jones); Page 21: Walter Iooss Jr. (Decker); Page 208: Mark Hanauer